CORPVS MONVMENTORVM
RELIGIONIS DEI MENIS
(CMRDM)

III
INTERPRETATIONS AND TESTIMONIA

ÉTUDES PRÉLIMINAIRES
AUX RELIGIONS ORIENTALES
DANS L'EMPIRE ROMAIN

PUBLIÉES PAR

M. J. VERMASEREN

TOME DIX-NEUVIÈME

EUGENE N. LANE

CORPVS MONVMENTORVM
RELIGIONIS DEI MENIS

(CMRDM)

III

INTERPRETATIONS AND TESTIMONIA

LEIDEN
E. J. BRILL
1976

EUGENE N. LANE

CORPVS MONVMENTORVM RELIGIONIS DEI MENIS
(CMRDM)

III

INTERPRETATIONS AND TESTIMONIA

WITH 2 PLATES

LEIDEN
E. J. BRILL
1976

ISBN 90 04 04516 3

Copyright 1976 by E. J. Brill, Leiden, Netherlands

All rights reserved. No part of this book may be reproduced or translated in any form, by print, photoprint, microfilm, microfiche or any other means without written permission from the publisher

PRINTED IN THE NETHERLANDS

γονεῦσι φιλτάτοις

CONTENTS

Preface	IX
I. The Attic Material Apart from the Sounion Inscriptions Including Material from the Aegean Islands	1
The Sounion Inscriptions	7
II. The Cult in Lydia	17
III. The Cult in Asia Minor, Apart from Lydia and Antioch in Pisidia	39
IV. The Cult at Antioch in Pisidia	55
V. The Epithets of Men and Other Adjectives Applied to Him	67
VI. Associations of Men with Other Divinities	81
VII. The Iconography of Men	99
VIII. The Worshippers of Men; Miscellaneous	109
Testimonia Antiqua	115
Addenda and Corrigenda to Volumes I and II	119
Addenda Ultima	122
Index	126
Concordance	132

PREFACE

In this the third and last volume of the *Corpus Monumentorum Religionis Dei Menis*, I intend to do three things. First, I will again present the literary testimonia concerning the cult. This requires no original work on my part: these testimonia have been presented several times before, most recently by myself, *Berytus*, 15, 1964, pp. 28-29 and 17, 1967-68, pp. 82-84. On the occasion of my first publication of the testimonia I made various comments about them with which I still find myself in substantial agreement. Since it would be fatuous to repeat them here, the reader is referred to the previous discussion.

Secondly, I will endeavor to interpret the collected material to some extent. In the process, I will try to draw together the information available from the inscriptions, from the coins, from the other representations in art, and from the testimonia. I will also try to draw together the information from different geographical areas. In general, I feel that the treatment of this cult in the past has suffered from fragmentation, something which impeded understanding, and I will do my best to rectify this shortcoming. I will also try to set the cult of Men in a more general socioreligious context. This, of course, is a job to which there would be no end, but the reader will note that I have particularly tried to relate Men-cult to that of Sarapis, as well as to the religious outlook which is betrayed in Aelius Aristides' *Hieroi Logoi*. In the course of the interpretation, I will discuss the various possibilities of restoration of those relatively few inscriptions concerning Men-cult in which such discussion is profitable. Thus I hope to fill in a deficiency which some critics have found in volume I, and which I think is best tackled only after a complete presentation of the evidence.

Finally, after a presentation of Addenda and Corrigenda to volumes I and II, I will present two indices, and thus, I hope, answer to another deficiency found by some critics. The first index will contain the *res et verba notabiliora* mentioned in the interpretative essay; the second will tell the reader where the various items catalogued in volumes I and II are discussed in the essay.

In addition to those thanked in the previous prefaces, I would like to take this opportunity to extend particular thanks to Mrs. R. H. Evelpides, Athens; Dr. Francesco Roncalli of the Vatican Museums; and Mr. H. Bartlett Wells of Washington, D.C., for their various contributions to the success of this project.

Columbia, Missouri　　　　　　　　　　　　　　　EUGENE N. LANE

CHAPTER ONE

THE ATTIC MATERIAL APART FROM THE SOUNION INSCRIPTIONS INCLUDING MATERIAL FROM THE AEGEAN ISLANDS

The Attic material, apart from the Sounion inscriptions, falls into two categories. The first comprises the epiphany reliefs, nos. 1, 2, 3, 4, and 10, as well as the altar, 8, and the statue base, 9. In this category also we can class the figurine, 14, from Eretria. The second category consists of the items 5, 6, and 7, and is generally dated later than the first.

The first category is generally dated early, well into the Hellenistic period, and thus presents us with the paradoxical fact that the earliest evidence for this Oriental cult is from mainland Greek soil. (The earliest securely datable evidence from Asia Minor that we so far have is the coin of Deiotarus of Galatia.[1]) With this first category are to be connected the Menagyrtai, apparently mendicant priests of Men, whom we have elsewhere discussed.[2] They remain rather shadowy, however, and no evidence has come to my attention since I wrote about them that casts any fuller light on them.

The material itself, although exiguous in comparison to what we have from Lydia, or from Antioch in Pisidia, is sufficient to establish certain generalities. In all the epiphany reliefs, Men appears oversize to a group of normal-sized worshippers. In nos. 1, 2, and 3, he is seated on a ram, in no. 10 on a large rooster, and on no. 14 he has at his feet what appears to be a panther.[3] On no. 4, the likeliest interpretation is that he is seated on a large crescent, as on no. 14, but it might be, if we had more of the relief, that it would turn out to be an animal. In all cases (except no. 3, where we have only an old drawing, and no. 14, which shows no worshippers), the wor-

[1] *CMRDM*, II, p. 151, Galatia 1.
[2] E. N. Lane, "A Re-Study of the God Men, III," *Berytus*, 17, 1968, p. 99.
[3] The one representation, no. 10, certainly does not justify the statement of Claireve Grandjouan, "But the cock-rider par excellence is Men," *The Athenian Agora*, VI, p. 13. Her identification of lamps with cock-rider as showing Men is to be rejected.

shippers are shown holding their right hands up to adore the god, in a gesture reminiscent of some of the Lydian material.[4] They are accompanied by a table, on which there are offerings of cakes of various kinds and shapes (sometimes very elaborate, e.g., no. 2) or perhaps fruit.[5] Men holds a patera (nos. 1, 10), or a staff (no. 4), both attributes well-known from the coin-representations. Except for no. 10, where the chicken appears as Men's mount, there are a pair of chickens, rooster and hen, on all other reliefs, either on or under the offering table. The reliefs portray couples (nos. 1, 4, 10) or more extended families (nos. 2, 3), thus implying a function of Men as protector of family life, perhaps god of fertility. This fact fits in well with the fact that no. 10 bears a specific dedication by a married couple, as do the altar, no. 8, and the statue base, no. 9. No. 10 has the form of a little building, and this fact may point to there being a shrine of Men where it was set up, as is the case with no. 2, also.[6] No. 8 would seem at first sight to point to a temple of Men in the Piraeus, with a priesthood, but L. Robert[7] equates the priestess of this inscription with a known ἱέρεια Γλαῦκον, priestess of the great mother, honored in 213/3 B.C.[8] The letter forms also appear to support that date.

Thus our inscription would have been set up in a temple of the great mother. No. 9, the statue base, also found in the Piraeus, would point to a shrine of some sort as its original location. The question arises concerning it, whether the word ἱερόν should be taken as referring to the statue,[9] or rather (with Foucart)[10] to the establishment of a shrine of Men. Unfortunately, the shape of the hole

[4] See below, p. 38.
[5] See below, p. 13-14, for our discussion of τράπεζα and ἔρανος in the Sounion inscriptions. Barbara Levick and A. M. Davies, in a discussion of the word κοπτοπώλης in no. 283 — Antioch in Pisidia, late III, A.D. — *Classical Review*, 85, 1971, p. 165, suggest that the profession of a pastry-maker is also relevant for our Attic material, although the inscriptions are widely separated in time and space. The relief of the *Koloenon katoikia* (see Ch. 2, n. 38) also seems to show cakes.
[6] Cf. the use of another form of aedicula in the material from Antioch in Pisidia.
[7] *BCH*, 60, 1936, p. 207, with further bibliographical citations.
[8] *IG*, II², 1314.
[9] Cf. *IGR*, III, 800.
[10] *BCH*, 4, 1880, p. 129.

does not tell us anything about the statue, whether it was a statue of Men, or of some other divinity or person dedicated to Men.[11]

As to the animals which appear with Men on these monuments, the chicken is one of his most faithful companions, appearing not only on these reliefs, but on the likewise Attic no. 6, on the terracotta presumably from Kula, no. 64, and on coins of Parlais and Prostanna, as well as on the Antiochene type of coin-representation at Antioch in Pisidia itself, and cities which copied the Antiochene type; likewise originally on no. 175, which is apparently a miniature of the Antiochene statue type which inspired the coin-representations. The ram is nowhere else associated with Men, although ram's heads appear as decoration on no. 85; and the panther on no. 14, if that is what it really is, is absolutely unique.[12]

As to the dating of these monuments, although it is generally given as early, hardly anything can be said with certainty. Nos. 2 and 3 have both been in private collections too long for anything to be known about the circumstances of their finding. G. Bakalakis assigns no. 2 a date of ca. 340 B.C., by comparison with the Mausoleum of Halicarnassus. The charioteer on the side opposite Men does indeed bear a strong resemblance to the charioteer of the Mausoleum frieze, but the Mausoleum could well have continued exerting its artistic influence for a long time after it was built, and I do not find the early dating necessarily convincing.[13]

Nos. 1 and 4 were both found in a disturbed context, the first built into a wall, the latter in a well. To nos. 9 and 10, the editors of the *IG²* assign a date "s. III a." with no explanation given, but Foucart gives an even earlier dating to no. 9 on the basis of letter forms.[14] No. 14 is said to have been found in a tomb of the third

---

[11] Cf. our nos. 34 and 86, as well as apparently 89. Also, in no. 28, a statue of Men is dedicated to Helios Men Kisauloddenos, and no. 84 is an equestrian statue of Men dedicated to Mother Plastene. In no. A9, a statue of Men is dedicated to the Demos, and no. 29 is apparently a statue base similar to the one we are dealing with here.

[12] For more discussion of these and other animals associated with Men, see below, p. 101-104.

[13] G. Bakalakis, *Hellenika Amphiglypha* (Diss., Thessaloniki, 1946), p. 67. For illustrations of the comparable material from the Mausoleum, see Rodenwalt, *Die Kunst der Antike*, Pl. 408.

[14] *BCH*, 4, 1880, p. 129: "Les lettres sont soignées et leur forme permet

century B.C., but no explanation is given, and the dating may be on the basis of the figurine, and thus circular.[15] Only in the case of no. 8 do we seem to be on solid ground, if we accept the identification of the priestess in it with the known priestess of the Mother of the Gods.[16]

Before we go on to consider the second category of Attic material, let us briefly examine other material of (at least apparent) Hellenistic date, namely the material from Delos (nos. 18 and 19) and from Rhodes (nos. 16 and 17). The two Delian inscriptions, both found in Sarapaea of the island, cannot really be dated except between the time of the introduction of the Egyptian cults into Delos, presumably at the end of the third century B.C.,[17] and the destruction of the island in the Mithradatic wars. Vidman[18] attributes both to the years before the Athenian colonization of 166 (almost all the material from Sarapaeum B is attributed to those years, whereas that from Sarapaeum C is split), but this seems arbitrary, and is dictated by nothing other than their inclusion in *IG* XI, rather than *Inscriptions de Délos*. This itself is nowhere explained except on the basis of letter forms, and that with hesitation, by Roussel.[19]

With the Rhodian inscriptions we are on even shakier ground. The religious colleges which honor people are a common feature of Rhodian epigraphy, and the *IG* XII devotes a whole section to inscriptions of this kind.[20] Hiller von Gaertringen does not attempt any date for our no. 16 in his edition of it.[21] Dittenberger, reprinting the inscription,[22] says "saec. II a," and P. M. Frazer[23] merely adds a question mark: "ii a.C.?" In fact there is no internal evidence for

de faire remonter jusqu'à la seconde moitié du quatrième siècle avant notre ère."

[15] *Archaiologikon Deltion*, 16, 1960, ii, p. 150.
[16] See notes 7 and 8 above.
[17] Roussel's note to *IG*, XI, 1299.
[18] *Sylloge Inscriptionum Religionis Isiacae et Sarapiacae* (= SIRIS), Berlin, 1969, nos. CE 34, CE 63.
[19] *Praefatio* to *IG*, XI, 4.
[20] *IG*, XII, i, 155-165.
[21] *IG*, XII, 1, 162.
[22] *SIG*³, 1114. He is echoed by Vidman, *SIRIS*, 76 ("saec. II a.").
[23] *Opuscula Atheniensia*, 3, 1960, p. 27, note 3.

dating this inscription, so far as I can see — "litteris sine cura inscriptis" — except that the four-bar sigma is still in use, and Rhodian dialecticisms are preserved. But this, *per se*, would only exclude it from the later empire; four-bar sigmas continue being used in the Lydian material well into the third century A.D., and dialecticisms continue until the end of antiquity. One must date it, if at all, by considerations of historical probability, such as wanting to see Egyptian gods (who are likewise mentioned) on Rhodes during the period of its maritime importance and close connections with Egypt, or by the context of other inscriptions which mention such colleges, and this context itself is none too strong.[24] I must renounce any attempt to provide a very accurate dating for our no. 16, and the same applies to our no. 17, which Hiller says to be inscribed "litteris crassis." Any time in the Hellenistic or even early Roman period seems quite possible. Likewise, only the most approximate of dates can be given to our no. 15, the corrupt inscription from Thasos. The letter forms C and ω point to the later imperial period, third century A.D., or later.

Turning now to the other Attic material, nos. 5, 6, and 7, we find it generally ascribed to a later date than the monuments of category 1, but again nothing can be said with certainty. No. 7, like the Delian material, shows the compatibility of the cult of Men with that of the Egyptian gods. It is a simple vow of thanks, for unspecified reason.[25] No information is available on the circumstances of the find. Vidman says, "saec. II-III p."[26] but one can probably specify that a little more and put it after the ConstitutionAntoniniana, as the dedicant is an Aurelius. The letters are C and ω, as in the Thasos inscription and the bulk of the Antiochene material, but the iota adscript is retained. The dedicant is a ἱερεὺς στολιστής of Isis and Sarapis, a free man; this office is known regularly in the Egyptian cult.[27]

---

[24] Cf. *IG*, XII, i, 157, which is dated by Hiller thus: "litteris summa cum cura confectis, quae primi a. Chr. n. saeculi comptam illam elegantiam redolent." Dating of inscriptions by smell does not seem very convincing to me.
[25] Cf. the use of εὐχαριστῶ in the Lydian material.
[26] *SIRIS*, 25.
[27] Vidman, *SIRIS*, 16, 17, and 25.

Nos. 5 and 6 are connected by the fact that they both give evidence for the connection of Men and Pan. No. 5 is a part of a well-head, together with an inscription referring to rainfall, fertility and superabundance. It gives us a tantalizing view of what might be expected of Men's divine activity.[28] The formula used is similar to the ὗε, κύε said by Proclus[29] to have been part of the Eleusinian mysteries, but is appropriate enough for any cult concerned with the fertility of man, crop, and beast. Leaving aside, however, the question of the content of the inscription, let us observe that the only indication of date is again from the letter forms, and that the curved ε would tend to put it at a late date, perhaps third century A.D. (The same letter form is used in the Antiochene dedications.) But nothing can be said with certainty. The *IG* merely says "aetate imperatorum."

No. 6 is even more elusive. It is distinctly an abnormal representation, to begin with. The three figures — Pan, Men, and a votary (as I believe, rather than a nymph) — are shown in a stylized cave, such as suits the worship of Pan. The workmanship is better than is normally found in monuments of this cult, and the figures are more naturalistically rendered, with less generalization. Men is lacking the Phrygian cap — this is a very rare phenomenon, paralleled only by a few other anomalous monuments, such as the baby-Men of no. 64 or the radiate Men of no. 142. But the rest of his clothing, the staff, chicken, and crescent suffice to identify him without question. The relief goes to show that the association with Pan is not restricted to the well-head, but the monument is just about impossible to date. Most people want to put it later than our category 1, but not too much later.[30]

[28] For Men's connection with water, cf. coin Nysa 29, which shows him as a river god. This will be discussed below, p. 107. The moon, with its supposed influence on weather (cf. Theophrastus, *On Weather Signs, passim*) would of course make Men a natural candidate for a fertility god.

[29] *In Timaeum*, 293. For signs of a special connection between Men and Demeter, see below, p. 83.

[30] Typical is S. Lauffer's vague remark, *Die Bergwerkssklaven von Laureion*, II, *Abhandlungen der Akademie der Wissenschaften und der Literatur in Mainz, Geistes- und Sozialwissenschaftliche Klasse*, 1956, 11, p. 44 (= 180) X, note 2: "Jünger als die Weihung aus Thorikos ist ... ein unbeschriftetes Relief mit Men, Pan, und einer Nymphe."

In sum, then, this material from mainland Greece and the islands is scattered not only in space but in time. Whereas the Sounion inscriptions seem datable to the late second century A.D., Attic category 1 would seem to group itself around no. 8, datable to the later third century B.C., and the Delian inscriptions are of the second century B.C. No. 5, no. 7, and the Thasian dedication no. 15 seem to date from the third century A.D., whereas no. 6 and the Rhodian inscriptions seem to me to be left floating anywhere in the Hellenistic or early Imperial periods, up to A.D. 200.

They show us not only about cult organizations in the worship of Men, but also about the association of Men and other divinities — Pan (5 and 6), Sarapis and Isis (7, 18, 19), and Dionysus (15). They show us Men as a god manifest and as a protector of family life, as well as a god with more general fertility powers, particularly connected with rainfall.

THE SOUNION INSCRIPTIONS

The Sounion inscriptions, nos. 11, 12, and 13, stand out from the mass of the Attic material in a number of ways. Not only are they apparently later than the bulk of the inscriptions of this area, although they can be dated only approximately in the late second century A.D., but they furnish us the most explicit information to be had on the procedural details of Men-worship anywhere.[31]

It is remarkable that these inscriptions, which have been mentioned in passing many times (my bibliography in *CMRDM*, I, barely scratches the surface in this case), have never been subjected

---

[31] Dittenberger, *SIG³*, no. 1042 dates no. 13 II-III A.D., without much conviction. For a while it seemed that there was an identification for Gaius Orbius, the owner of the slave Xanthus who founded the sanctuary. See J. H. Oliver, *Hesperia*, 32, 1963, p. 318; Robert, *REG*, 77, 1964, p. 156, no. 138. Oliver would like to identify him with the archon of 186/7 A.D., whose name he said should be restored as Γ. ['Ορ]βίου Θισβιαν[οῦ] of Marathon in an inscription first published by Raubitschek, *Hesperia*, Suppl. VII, 1951, p. 279. This identification, however, has now vanished. Publication of a photograph by G. Manganaro, *Archaelogia Classica*, 16, 1964, p. 294, showed the name to be Φάβιον. For the most recent discussion see J. H. Oliver, *Zeitschrift für Papyrologie und Epigraphik*, 14, 1974, p. 137.

8   THE ATTIC MATERIAL

to a really close examination, and that prior to the time of *CMRDM*, I, no photographs of them had ever appeared.

The cult-regulations exist in two copies, which were accompanied by a simple dedication (no. 11, now lost) by Xanthus to Men Tyrannus.[32] It is fairly obvious that inscription 13 is a later version of inscription 12, but not because the language has been cleaned up or debarbarized in no. 13, as some authorities claim.[33] Rather it is simply because the space provided on the stele used for no. 12 was inadequate. Not only are the regulations of no. 12 considerably abbreviated by comparison with those of no. 13, but even so they inconveniently spill over onto the side of the stone, on which the last four words are uncomfortably incised. Subsequently, no. 13 was inscribed, giving more complete regulations and not running off the room provided, but hardly more careful in grammar or spelling, and, if anything, with even more carelessly formed letters.

Under a crescent moon, in both cases, we first hear how Xanthus the Lycian, slave of Gaius Orbius, founded a temple of Men Tyrannus, αἱρετίσαντος τοῦ θεοῦ. That is to say, the god chose him somehow to found this temple. How? Again, as in the case of the Lydian inscriptions (which we will discuss in the next chapter), we have to assume direct communication of some sort between god and man.[34] Our phrase here stands in the same position as the phrase κατ' ἐπιταγήν so often found in the Lydian material, but as usual the

---

[32] F. Bömer makes the point, *Untersuchungen über die Religion der Sklaven in Griechenland und Rom*, Abhandlungen der Akademie der Wissenschaften und der Literatur in Mainz, Geistes- und Sozialwissenschaftliche Klasse, 1961, 4, p. 199 (= 441), that *tyrannos* is particularly appropriate for a slave-cult. Slaves were allowed into these non-state cults more readily than into the official ones. This disregards, however, the fact that Men was very much the object of a state-cult in some parts of Asia Minor, as evidenced by the coins. Bömer is also at pains, pp. 438-9, to deny slave status to the dedicants of our 8, 9, and 10, and prefers to see them as free metics. It should be noted that all these people seem to be married couples. Bömer likewise gives general reflections on the implications of such a title as *tyrannos*, p. 448. The view that Men-worshippers in Attica were primarily slaves is fostered, not only by Martin Nilson, but particularly by S. Lauffer, *op. cit.*, p. 179 (= 943). We will return to this point later, p. 109 below.

[33] E.g., Dittenberger in his commentary to *SIG*³, 1042.

[34] Note also that the commonest form of Attic relief shows some sort of epiphany of the god.

means of the god's command are not specified.[35] It is curious that Xanthus is a Lycian, from an area of Asia Minor where Men-worship has not yet been attested. One cannot put too much weight on this, however, as new material[36] has just in recent years brought us attestations of Men-worship from new areas, but if Men remains unattested in Lycia, it can always be supposed that Xanthus became familiar with the cult in some other area of Asia Minor, or even in Attica itself, as the cult had been long established there. The purpose of the temple seems mostly to be for private sacrifices (reminding one of the rural sanctuary of Pan in Menander's *Dyscolus*), presumably of cattle.[37] Nowhere is it stated in the Xanthus inscriptions, however, what the motive for sacrificing might be, and the absence of votive inscriptions from this sanctuary speaks loudly that here, as opposed to Lydia, for example, one did not pray or sacrifice to Men for specific purposes, but merely to gain the general good-will of the god: εὐείλατος γένοιτο ὁ θεὸς τοῖς θεραπεύουσιν ἁπλῇ τῇ ψυχῇ[38]; εὐείλατος γένοιτο ὁ θεὸς τοῖς ἁπλῶς προσπορευομένοις.[39] I will return to the matter of sacrifices later on, but first let us turn our attention to the subject which occupies nearly all of no. 12 and the first part of no. 13: ritual cleanliness.

This is the only document of Men-worship in which prescriptions for ritual cleanliness are spelled out, although the καταλουστικοί of the Lydian inscriptions[40] may have had something to do with the same sort of situation. It is interesting to see what the prohibited items are. In no. 12, lines 9-11, we read: καθαριζέστω δὲ ἀπὸ σκόρδων καὶ χοιρέων and later, lines 23-25, ἀπὸ δὲ γυναικὸς λουσάμενοι κατακέφαλα αὐθειμερί. In no. 13, this has been brought together, lines 3-5:

---

[35] The phrase ἐπ' ἀγαθῇ τύχῃ which appears here, although extremely common in epistolary inscriptions, occurs in Men-material only here and in no. A7, a dedication of an altar at Kalburcu, near the ancient Nicomedeia.

[36] Nos. A5, A6, and A7.

[37] Cf. the bulls tied to altars in the Antiochene material, nos. 177 and 288, and the bull which was the intended offering of the dedicant of the Lydian inscription, no. 50. The ox, often merely a bucranium, is one of the commonest attributes of Men, not only on the monuments, but especially on the coins. See below, p. 102-103.

[38] No. 12, lines 25-26.

[39] No. 13, line 12.

[40] Nos. 34, A3.

καθαριζέστω δὲ ἀπὸ σκόρδων κα[ὶ χοιρέων] καὶ γυναικός, λουσαμένους δὲ κατακέφαλα αὐθημερὸν εἰσ[πορεύ]εσθαι. (Note the implication that there were primarily male worshippers, something not normal for Men-cult.) The first three things, then, considered unclean are garlic, pork, and sexual relations, although the miasma can be removed by bathing, and the worshipper can enter the temple the same day. In spite of its age, the standard work on the subject of ancient ritual cleanliness is still that of Th. Wächter.[41] He discusses[42] garlic among forbidden foods, and cites as parallel a passage of Athenaeus, (X, 422 D), concerning the prohibition of garlic from a temple of the mother of the gods. The prohibition of swine, however, is much more general, and Wächter is able to cite several such instances, particularly from the cult of Aphrodite.[43] For abstension from sexual relations, the parallels are given by another old but still standard work, this time by Eugen Fehrle.[44] He cites this passage and quotes this inscription among many parallels.[45] Fehrle's basic thesis is that sexual contact between humans stands in the way of divine contact between god and humans, and that consequently chastity brings man closer to god and gives him supernatural powers.[46] It is beyond the scope of this work to go into these psychological speculations; suffice it to say that in the cult of Men, chastity seems not to be an important consideration, because the miasma of sex is able to be removed so quickly and so easily. More serious are uncleannesses that might seem to result from the more mysterious forces of nature, incomprehensible aspects of existence. A woman is supposed to wait seven days after her menstrual period (that, in itself, easily enough connected with a god of the moon) and then wash and come in the same day (12, line 20; 13, line 5-6; this stands in contradiction to the apparent male-dominance of the

---

[41] *Reinheitsvorschriften im griechischen Kultus*, RGVV, IX, i, 1910.

[42] *Op. cit.*, p. 105. The reference involves Stilpo, a fourth century B.C. philosopher of the Megarian school.

[43] *Op. cit.*, pp. 82-87. The uncleanness of pork in Judaism, etc., is too much of a commonplace to require mentioning.

[44] *Die kultische Keuschheit im Altertum*, RGVV, VI, 1910.

[45] Cites passage, *op. cit.*, p. 26; quotes entire inscription, p. 137.

[46] *Op. cit.*, p. 65. The importance of celibacy in Christianity hardly needs to be mentioned.

cult). According to Wächter's parallels, this is something rare. He is able to quote only one parallel, that from a temple of Asclepius in Ptolemais of Egypt.[47] In both these cases, the period set for cleansing is seven days, or one quarter of the moon. From contact with a dead person, the period is set at ten days (12, lines 19-20; 12, line 6). The idea that the dead cause pollution is a common conception, and Wächter is able to cite many parallels,[48] the best-known being the prohibition of the dead from Apollo's sacred island of Delos. Even stronger is the prohibition against a murderer (11, line 21: ἀνδροφόνον μηδὲ περὶ τὸν τόπον), although curiously the provision is omitted in no. 12.[49]

Finally, a forty-day long delay is imposed after φθορά,[50] to be interpreted as a voluntary abortion or involuntary miscarriage. Wächter treats this as part of the general uncleanness regarding birth (in present-day Greece, women are still traditionally not supposed to venture out of the house until forty days have passed after a normal birth) and is able to draw specific parallels between the uncleanness of birth and the uncleanness of death, both from the temple at Ptolemais, which has been mentioned, and from Lindos. In all cases the unclean period is forty days.[51]

The main provision, however, which is emphasized in both inscriptions (12, line 26; 13, lines 12 and 26) is purity of soul (ἁπλῇ τῇ ψυχῇ) and that seems to sum up all the particular ritual purifications.[52] No particular mention is made of priesthoods or other cult-personnel, except that the founder of the temple (μηθένα θυσιάζειν ἄνευ τοῦ καθιδρουσαμένου, 12, lines 11-13; 13, lines 7-8) or

---

[47] Wächter, *op. cit.*, p. 36.
[48] *Op. cit.*, p. 55 ff.
[49] I do not think, however, that it would be safe to conclude with Gurlitt, *Philologus*, 27, 1868, pp. 729-735, that this meant the cult was now opened up even for murderers. Ziehen seems to be on a better track, *Leges Graecorum Sacrae*, II, 1, p. 151, in thinking a regulation against murderers obvious and superfluous, therefore omitted.
[50] See particularly J. Ilberg, *Archiv für Religionswissenschaft*, 13, 1910, p. 1 ff.; S. Wide, *ARW*, 12, 1909, p. 4 ff.
[51] Mentioned by Gurlitt, *art. cit.*, p. 722; Wide, *art. cit.*, also has some comment on the number forty.
[52] See Wide, *art. cit.*, for biblical parallels both to the vocabulary and the tabus of this inscription. See also Bömer, *op. cit.*, 118 (= 440) for a discussion of purity of soul.

his appointed lieutenant (ἐὰν δέ τινα ἀνθρώπινα πάσχῃ ἢ ἀσθενήσῃ ἢ ἀποδημήσῃ, θεραπευέ[τω] τὸν θεὸν ὧι ἂν αὐτὸς παραδοῖ, 12, lines 27-29; 13, lines 12-14) must be present at a sacrifice to get their own (the god's) share of the victim.[53] If anyone violates this regulation, however, there is no particular penalty invoked, except that the sacrifice is unacceptable to the god (ἀπρόσδεκτος ἡ θυσία παρὰ τοῦ θεοῦ, 12, line 14; 13, lines 8-9).

There must, however, have been certain secret cult implements or the like, because curiosity or meddling with them is subject to more drastic sanctions (12, lines 28-31; 13, lines 14-16): ὃς ἂν δὲ πολυπραγμονήσῃ τὰ τοῦ θεοῦ ἢ περιεργάσηται, ἁμαρτίαν ὀφειλέτω Μηνὶ Τυράννῳ, ἣν οὐ μὴ δύνηται ἐξειλάσασθαι.[54]

The sacrifices seem to fall into various categories:
1. A regular sacrifice. This presumably can be done only from the new moon to the fifteenth of the month, according to the afterthought of 13, lines 18-20. It appears that the sacrificer could retain most of the sacrificial meat, but had to furnish the god the appropriate parts — the right haunch, the hide, the head (only in no. 13), the feet (also only in no. 13), and the chest.[55] These parts were apparently kept and put to use by Xanthus, although the exact usefulness of the head and feet appear minimal to me. Furthermore, the sacrificer was to furnish oil for the altar, a lamp,[56] and kindling[57] (only in no. 13), as well as a libation. The details give us some idea of the procedure for the sacrifice. I would imagine that both the oil and the kindling would be used to get the fire going under the part of the animal to be burnt (maybe it is here that the feet and the head come in, instead of being retained by Xanthus), and that the

---

[53] Gurlitt, *art. cit.*, p. 732; Ziehen, *op. cit.*, II, i, p. 152; Lauffer, *op. cit.*, p. 183 (= 947).

[54] Cf. the use of ἁμαρτία and ἐξειλάσκομαι in the Lydian inscriptions, as well as of the adjective εὐείλατος in these very Sounion inscriptions.

[55] The word used here, στηθύνιον, could apparently also mean a part of the feet, according to the commentary in *IG*, II². References are given to Ziehen, *op. cit.*, II, i, 48, p. 149 note 4 and to Hesychius, *s.v.*

[56] Lamps are well known as offerings to the gods from the Roman period, e.g., in the Cretan cave-cult and in the Fountain of Peirene at Corinth. Bibliography is given by Thomas Kraabel, *GRBS*, 10, 1969, p. 90, note 41.

[57] For σχίζας see L. Robert, *American Studies in Papyrology*, I, 1966, p. 199, note 150.

libation would be poured over the sacrificial fire.

2. No. 13 is more explicit about other types of sacrifice. On the seventh of the month, the first quarter of the moon, a special sacrifice seems to have been called for. On this occasion one not only pays τὸ καθῆκον to the god, but τὰ καθήκοντα πάντα (no. 13, line 16 ff.). The sacrificer receives only the haunch and shoulder of the sacrifice he brings, the rest being cut up in the temple.[58] The rest of the procedure is left unclear. Inasmuch as this sacrifice involves a much greater material loss for the sacrificer, it is to be assumed that there must be a particular divine advantage to be gained from sacrificing at the first quarter.

3. Another possible offering to Men is described by the word τράπεζα (no. 13, line 20). All in all the idea of a table plays an important part in the cult of Men and certain other cults and a thorough treatment is given in an article by Barbara Levick.[59] We have the following evidence:

a) The tables with offerings to Men shown on the Attic reliefs, 1, 2, 3, 4, and 10.

b) The so-called altar of Men shown on the reverses of coins of Attouda (our Attouda 1, but also several coins which do not have Men as obverse type).

c) The table dedicated to Men by Protion, our no. 255.[60]

d) The table which apparently existed in the side-building of the temple of Men on Kara Kuyu outside Pisidian Antioch.[61]

e) More tangentially related to Men-cult, the sacred table mention-

---

[58] Κατακόπτεται. The commentary of *IG*, II², referring to Ziehen, *op. cit.*, p. 152, no. 21 and to Stengel, *Hermes*, 39, 1904, p. 616, says that the word can have the meaning "consumed."

[59] *JHS*, 91, 1971, p. 80 ff. In this article, Miss Levick assumes, however, that the τράπεζα and the ἔρανος of this inscription are the same thing, something of which I am not convinced. The phrase λαμβανέτω τὸ ἥμισυ cannot be equated with the phrase ὁμοίως δὲ παρέξουσιν κτλ. Also the ἔρανος seems to have included blood-offerings. These considerations would give that much less reason than even Miss Levick sees for assuming any connection between these holy tables and the presumed common meals of the Xenoi Tekmoreioi.

[60] If a connection can be made with the Protion who made the dedication of the βωμός of our no. 163, then the likelihood is that this table was located in a wayside shrine. I opt for the third of the possibilities listed by Levick, *art. cit.*, p. 84.

[61] Ramsay's stones of initiation. See Lane, *Berytus*, 15, 1964, p. 41.

ed among the offerings in the temple of Helios Apollo Kisauloddenos in Smyrna (our no. 28) only one line after the statue of Men is mentioned.

f) The tables mentioned among other furniture offered by a paredros of Men in our no. 121.[62]

Levick observes[63] that the table, as opposed to the altar, was intended for bloodless offerings, and this seems borne out by the objects, unidentifiable though they are in detail, appearing on the table in the Attic reliefs. They would seem to be cakes of various sorts, and perhaps fruit.

I think, then, that it would be safe to conclude that the table mentioned in this inscription, and probably also the table dedicated by Protion, were used for bloodless offerings. In this case, the dedicant was to receive half, the other half going to the god, or to his ministers.

4. It seems to me that the ἔρανος mentioned in no. 13, lines 21-26, is an entirely different matter from the τράπεζα mentioned above, involving both bloody and bloodless sacrifices, although as we shall see, there are some possible points of similarity.[64] Although we do not seem to be dealing with a permanent organization here, we are still in the framework of communal worship that is familiar from the δοῦμος and the καταλουστικοί of the Lydian material, the Μηνιασταί of the Rhodian inscriptions, and perhaps the Ξένοι Τεκμόρειοι of the area of Antioch, if their relation to Men-cult is more than merely tangential.[65] The ἔρανος is open to all who wish to join in it. The ἐρανισταί are also to furnish τὰ καθήκοντα to the god, making this a sacrifice of the more elaborate kind, like that on the seventh of the month, and if they lay down at the banquet — apparently a particularly lavish sort of thing for people of this low station — there were even further offerings for them to make.

[62] Mentioned by Levick, *art. cit.*, p. 84. Cf. also no. 119 in which a table is dedicated by a priest of Men to Herakles and the people.

[63] *Art. cit.*, p. 82. H. Mischkowski, *Die heiligen Tische im Götterkultus der Griechen und Römer*, Diss., Königsberg, 1917, pp. 38-39, is of the opinion that by eating off of the god's table, the worshipper consumes food which he has blessed.

[64] For similar ἐρανισταί cf. Ziehen, *op. cit.*, II, i, p. 147, note 47.

[65] See Levick, *art. cit.*, pp. 83-84. There will be more discussion of this matter below when we deal with the cult at Antioch in Pisidia.

Unfortunately the right side of the last part of this inscription is broken away, and we are dealing here with one of the relatively few instances in all the epigraphical evidence concerning Men, in which the reading of the inscription is neither virtually assured nor virtually hopeless, and in which there are various possibilities which have been suggested for the restoration of the ends of these lines.[66]

The simple ἐρανισταί like the simple sacrificer, are supposed to supply the δεξιόν σκέλος and δορά, as well as a specific amount of oil (κοτύλην ἐλαίου), and a likewise specified amount of wine (χοῦν οἴνου), presumably for the libation. Instead, however, of the lamp and kindling, they are supposed to furnish the following bloodless offerings:

a) Ἐφίερα τρία. Although Sokolowski[67] thinks of supplements to the sacrifice, the consensus seems to be that this is a kind of sacrificial cake.[68] The context of this inscription would lend support to this definition.

b) Κολλύβων χοίνικες δύο. Again, the reference seems to be to some kind of small cake. But this word, which occurs rarely in Ancient Greek, is the regular term for the offerings still placed in present-day Greece at the tombs of the dead, and then consumed by the church congregation.[69] We can only speculate whether this offering may not have some bearing on Μὴν Καταχθόνιος, protector of graves in Lycaonia.[70]

c) Most mysterious of all are the other two offerings, as the text is uncertain. The *IG*², followed by Sokolowski, supplies να[στὸν χοινι]κιαῖον in the first lacuna, whereas Dittenberger, in his publication for *SIG*, suggested νό[μισμα οὐγ]κιαῖον. As far as I can

---

[66] The text that I reprinted in *CMRDM*, I, is that of the *IG*². A convenient apparatus is given by F. Sokolowski, *Lois sacrées des cités grecques*, Paris, 1969, p. 107.

[67] *Op. cit.*, p. 14, commenting on the phrase τὰ ἐφ' ἱεροῖς in a calendar from Eleusis of the late fourth century B.C.

[68] Cf. *LSJ*, s.v.; in Sokolowski, *op. cit.*, *Supplement*, Paris, 1962, no. 92, line 5 there are also apparently cakes called τὰ ἐφίερος (Ialysos, ca. 200 B.C.). Pollux, *Onomasticon*, VI, 76, gives ἐφίερος in a list of types of μᾶζαι.

[69] See Schmidt, *ARW*, 25, 1927, 52 ff. For occurrences of the word in Ancient Greek see *LSJ*, s.v.

[70] See Lauffer, *op. cit.*, p. 181 (= 945), who would like to see a connection of Μὴν Καταχθόνιος with his worship by mineworkers.

determine from the photograph, the traces on the stone — all letters in this inscription are scrawled — suggest α rather than ο. Furthermore, ναστός, yet another kind of cake, fits the context better than Dittenberger's supplement, which would assume a cash payment to Xanthus for banqueters to use his sanctuary.[71] Finally, although I think that the τράπεζα and the ἔρανος are essentially different things, there is no reason why we should not identify the three kinds of cake apparently mentioned with the various cakes that appear on the earlier Attic reliefs.

d) The final offering has much baffled scholars. We, following *IG*, wrote ἀκρό[αμα], and Dittenberger, following Ziehen, apparently abandoned his original ἀκρο[θίνιον] for ἀκρο[άματα] (plural). He defends this[72] by reference to a decree of Magnesia on the Maeander, dated 196 A.D., defining the functions of the στεφανηφόρος on the occasion of the feast of Zeus Sosipolis.[73] This official is to provide ἀκροάματα αὐλητὴν συριστὴν κιθαριστήν. I cannot say that I am happy with this interpretation based on a large public festival, here at a very modest sanctuary. I cannot quite see concerts by distinguished instrumentalists, although perhaps, again on the parallel of Menander, a few flute-girls might be in order.

The other possible restorations that have been suggested are: ἀκρο[θίνιον], "firstfruits" (Dittenberger); ἀκρο[κώλια], "the extremities of the sacrificed animal" (Foucart), apparently out of place here among the list of bloodless offerings, but things are not necessarily put in logical order in these inscriptions; and ἀκρό[δρυα], "hard-shelled fruits" (Sokolowski). Although Sokolowski offers no explanation of his suggestion, it is perhaps to be preferred over the others in terms of the context and of the representations on reliefs.

Lastly, we must note that the banqueters who recline at tables are to offer the god a wreath, as well as wreathing themselves, and are to add a woollen fillet or ribbon to hang from it. The assumption then is, I think, that the god is seen as joining in the banquet along with his worshippers.

[71] There are admittedly sanctuaries of Men which seem to have attached considerable importance to money, particularly that of no. 121.

[72] *SIG*³, II, p. 197.

[73] *SIG*³, no. 589, line 45. Ἀκροάματα are discussed by L. Robert, *Hermes*, 65, 1930, p. 116.

CHAPTER TWO

THE CULT IN LYDIA

The cult of Men in Lydia poses certain problems which are not encountered elsewhere. These problems are both posed, and partially solved, by the relative explicitness of the inscriptions, some of which, *e.g.*, no. 44, amount to little narratives. Yet there is much in them which is taken for granted, and must have been obvious to contemporaries, but barring new discoveries must remain obscure to the present-day scholar.

The area around Kula is so rich in material concerning Men and the divinities associated with him, that there can be little doubt but that several sanctuaries of this divinity existed there in the early centuries of our era.[1] The earliest securely datable document, no. 56, is from 66-67 A.D., and the latest, no. 65, although the date is not legible with certainty, seems to be from 269-70 A.D. It is in these sanctuaries, so far untouched by the archaeologist's spade, that the votive inscriptions were set up, that the procedures described in them were carried out, and that dedications to Men were made. In Ayazviran[2] a sanctuary is specifically known to have existed, as in no. 44 the appeal to the god to adjudicate the dispute is specifically said to have taken place ἐν τῷ ναῷ, and no. 49 is a βωμός, probably dedicated in the same sanctuary, and now preserved in the local mosque. Furthermore, if we are to trust the corrupt no. 52, presumably found in Menye, a πρόπυλον was dedicated to Men in a sanctuary there. We also know from no. 79 that Men had a temple in Sardis, a place which from the general tenor of the dedications is part of this area in a religious sense.

Many of the votive inscriptions are simple, and merely record a prayer made by someone, its being answered by the god, and the thankfulness of the worshipper. Things that can be prayed for are

[1] Cf. L. Robert, *Anatolia*, 3, 1958, p. 122 = *Opera Minora Selecta*, I, p. 421, "Les campagnes de la Méonie semblent avoir été parsemés de petits sanctuaires ruraux des dieux locaux."

[2] Which in *CMRDM*, I, I was too hasty in identifying with ancient Koresa. See my article in *Anatolian Studies*, 25, 1975, pp. 109-110.

parts of the body (eyes, no. 32[3]; feet, nos. 59 and 65; breast, no. 74; breast, legs and eyes, no. 35; a leg, no. 31) or a mule (no. 37). The prayers can be made on one's own behalf, on behalf of one's children (nos. 33, 35, 63, 65, 68, 72, A2), one's foster children (nos. 35, 39, 40, 41)[4], or one's brothers (no. 50). Or one can pray to get a wife (no. 80). Others yet do not tell us the reason for the vow, merely that the prayer was successful (nos. 45, 46, 60).

The vocabulary for these simple votive inscriptions is usually uncomplicated, provided that no unusual circumstances set in. They usually end in (εὐχὴν) ἀνέστησα or ἀνέθηκα, with variations of person and number, sometimes with the addition of forms of εὐχαριστῶ (nos. 45, 46, 60)[5] or εὐλογῶ (nos. 65, 68, 80). Twice only among these inscriptions does the concept of σωτηρία, common farther east, come out (nos. 41 — if Buresch's restoration is correct — and no. 72).[6]

Nos. 45 and 60 apparently belong to this category of simple vows, but are distinguished by the phrase ἀπέδωκαν τὸ ἱεροποίημα and thus resemble no. 35 (which will be analyzed later) which uses the phrase ποιήσαντες τὸ ἱεροποίημα. Ἀπέδωκαν of course, has the idea of giving back, as if the ἱεροποίημα or vow (εὐχή, no. 63) were a *quid pro quo*, given back to the god in return for his granting a favor. Although ἱεροποίημα would seem on the basis of no. 63 to be an equivalent expression for εὐχή, it is distinctly a peculiarity of the inscriptions of this area, and seems to have no particular connection with the known office of ἱεροποιός.[7] Apart from these three inscriptions, I know it only from one other inscription of the area,[8] which, along

---

[3] For eye trouble in general in the inscriptions of this area, see P. Herrmann, *Ergebnisse einer Reise in Nordostlydien, Denkschriften der österreichischen Akademie der Wissenschaften, Phil.-Hist. Klasse*, 80, 1962, note 202.

[4] See below for the importance of θρεπτοί at Antioch in Pisidia. The well-known contemporary orator and religious maniac, Aelius Aristides, constantly refers with affection to his foster *parents*, τροφεῖς.

[5] For thanking the god, see L. Robert, *Hellenica*, 10, 1955, p. 55 ff. Possible variants on this idea are no. 31 (ἐπὶ χάριτος), and even no. 15, from Thasos, if the reading of the end of the inscription is to be trusted (Λαέου χάριν [ποιοῦ]σα). It could be that a form of the verb εὐχαριστῶ is lurking in the corruption here.

[6] For examples from farther east, cf. nos. 88, 91, 92, 105, 107, 142, and A6.

[7] See *LSJ*, s.v.

[8] Zingerle, *Jahreshefte des österreichischen archäologischen Instituts*, 23,

with no. 35 complicates the situation and makes it appear that a ἱεροποίημα is more than a mere vow. Franz Steinleitner, one of the foremost students of these inscriptions, refuses to equate ἱεροποίημα with στήλη or ἀνάθημα, but rather defines it as the pleasing of the god through the erection of the stele, or whatever the case called for.[9] He seems to me to be on the right track.

In the inscription which we mentioned above as providing a parallel for the use of this unusual word, although the god addressed is Anaeitis alone, the situation, whatever the exact meaning of the text, is similar to that of some of the Men-inscriptions which will be discussed later. In it, an offense has been committed against the god (ἡμάρτησεν), and she demanded the ἱεροποίημα as propitiation (εἰλασάμενος). Similar seems to be the situation in no. 35, where a whole group of people seem to be afflicted in various parts of the body. Although no ἁμαρτία is mentioned, no. 35 differs from nos. 45 and 60, as well as from other vows involving parts of the body, in that it is felt necessary to propitiate (εἰλασάμενυ) the god in order to obtain relief from sickness. Obviously the implication is that the sickness was visited on the sufferers as a result of an unknown offense.

Compare no. 77, with its phrase: ἀμ[αρτήσας κα]ταπίπτω εἰς ἀ[σθένειαν] καὶ ὁμολογῶ τ[ὸ ἁμάρτημ]α. Although the inscription is so heavily restored as not to be entirely reliable, its editors, Josef Keil and Anton von Premerstein, obviously had a case similar to, but more explicit than no. 35 in mind.[10]

Also noteworthy in no. 35 is the fact that the record of these

---

1926, Beiblatt, col. 28, no. 5: Steinleitner, *Die Beicht im Zusammenhange mit der sakralen Rechtspflege in der Antike*, Munich, 1913, no. 5; see H. W. Pleket, *Greek Inscriptions in the Rijksmuseum van Oudheden at Leiden*, Oudheidkundige Mededeelingen, Suppl. to vol. 38, p. 85, note 2). I give the text of Steinleitner and Pleket here: Μεγάλη Ἀνάειτις. Ἐπεὶ ἡμάρτησεν Φορβος, ἐπεζήτησεν ἱερο[π]όημα. Ἀποδεί(δει) νῦν εἰλασάμενος καὶ εὐχαριστῶν. Ἔτους σνδ΄, μη(νὸς) Ἀρτεμισίου β΄.

[9] Steinleitner, *op. cit.*, p. 25-26, and again, taking issue with Buresch, p. 113, note 3.

[10] If Buckler and Robinson's restoration [ἐλεη]θείς is to be trusted, then the sin was doubly bad, coming after previous mercy from the god, a characteristic unknown except for no. 50. Buckler and Robinson also suggest σωθείς or ἰαθείς as possibilities, but the basic idea would remain the same.

actions is called an ἔνγραφον, as opposed to the more normal word, στηλογραφῶ.[11]

Two others of these "simple" dedications also turn out not to be so simple after all, but to have further implications. The first of these is no. 50, in which Men appears for the only time as an accommodating, forgiving god. In this story of a girl who prayed for her brothers, but was unable to give the bull which she had rashly promised, Men agreed to accept the stele instead. We hear here also, as in no. 47, which will be discussed later, of a worshipper being able to ask a divinity a question and receive an answer. How this took place, whether through a human priest as an intermediary,[12] or through prayer and vision,[13] we can only conjecture. We will have occasion to return to this question later on.[14]

The second of these inscriptions which turn out not to be so simple after all is no. 80. Men was not always so nice as in no. 50 to those who failed to keep their vows to him. In this case, Epaphrodeitos had prayed to Men to receive the wife of his choice, but had not kept his vow. As a result he was punished (κολασθείς) in an unspecified manner, and belatedly paid the vow (εὐλογῶ — this word is regularly used in the so-called *Sühneninschriften* and in some of the thanksgiving ones as well).[15]

In this inscription, the god punished an offense against himself, namely failure to keep a vow. Let us now examine another inscription (no. 47), in which Men likewise punishes an offense against himself. In this inscription, Trophime, daughter of Artemidorus, is called into an unspecified service (ὑπηρεσία) by the god, but fails to appear quickly. She is then caused to go mad (μανῆναι). So she asks Mother Tarsene and Apollo Tarsios and Men Artemidorou Axiottenos, and is instructed to enroll (καταγράψαι) herself into the

[11] Cf. Buckler, *Annual of the British School at Athens*, 21, 1914-16, p. 169, no. 1, ἐνέγραψα.
[12] Of human priests as intermediaries we hear very little in this area. Cf. Herrmann, *op. cit.*, p. 25, note 83.
[13] Cf. the phrase δι' ἀγγέλου in no. 69.
[14] Cf. Steinleitner, *op. cit.*, no. 18, from Philadelphia Lydiae: Αὐρήλιος Τρόφιμος ἐρωτήσα(ς) τὸν θεὸν ἀνέστησα Μητρὶ Θεῶν.
[15] Cf. Herrmann, *op. cit.*, no. 50 — a prayer to Zeus Peizenos on behalf of an ox, not kept, had as result eye trouble for the worshipper's daughter; cf. also Steinleitner, *op. cit.*, no. 33.

service of the god.[16] In this inscription, there is much that remains unclear. Totally apart from the variation of the divinity from the singular to the plural and back again, we do not know exactly how Trophime was called (κληθεῖσα) by the god, or into what kind of service. There is also the unclear matter of asking the god and receiving an answer, which we discussed previously in regard to no. 50. One may speculate that the service required was that of a ἱερόδουλος (the word has a wide range of meanings, from literal to euphemistic), and it is true that ἱερόδουλοι are attested in a few monuments from this area.[17] But this remains sheer speculation. Interesting also in this inscription is the use of the word νέμεσις (cf. no. 69) for the more normal κόλασις or the like.[18]

Another important idea in this group of inscriptions is that of λύτρον. This word obviously has "ransom" as its basic meaning,[19] and its clearest usage (leaving aside for the moment the other

[16] For parallels, see Buckler, art. cit., p. 169, no. 1 — an offense against Zeus Sabazios and Mother Hipta as a result of stealing sacred pigeons, and Herrmann, op. cit., no. 45, and offense against the same divinities by dragging off a ἱερόδουλος. Both end in punishments in the eyes. Eyes were also among the stricken parts of the body in our no. 35. Cf. also Sardis, VII, i, no. 95.

[17] See Herrmann, op. cit., no. 45, for a male ἱερόδουλος of Sabazius and Mother Hipta. Cf. also Steinleitner, op. cit., no. 15. Ἱερόδουλοι are mentioned among Men-related material in the temple of Helios Apollo Kisauloddenos (no. 28), apparently of the 1st century A.D. We know also from Strabo's references that temples of Men elsewhere had such temple slaves: the temple of Men Pharnakou had πολλοὺς ἱεροδούλους (XII, 3, 31 = T. 1) and that at Pisidian Antioch had a πλῆθος ἱεροδούλων prior to the time of Augustus (XII, 8, 14 = T. 2). Lydia is of course known from Herodotus to have been a center of temple-prostitution, but at a much earlier time.

[18] For another case of an offense against a god being punished, cf. Steinleitner, op. cit., no. 13 (Archäologische Zeitung, 38, 1880, p. 38; Staatliche Museen zu Berlin, Beschreibung der antiken Skulpturen, Berlin, 1891, no. 680) in which Apollo Bozenos punished a girl for going to a dance in dirty clothing. Parallels for this sort of thing are to be found in Wächter, Reinheitsvorschriften, p. 15. Ramsay takes χορόν to be a misspelling for χωρίον, and interprets the word as meaning a holy village, or the like, Cities and Bishoprics of Phrygia, Oxford, 1895, I, p. 152. In this he is followed by Steinleitner and Wächter, but the emendation does not seem to me to be called for. Again, Ramsay is forcing evidence into a preconceived theory, this time that of temple-estates. A photo of this inscription is given, Robert, Hellenica, 3, 1946, Pl. 4.

[19] Cf. Herrmann, op. cit., p. 40, note 185 for various forced meanings that scholars have tried to give the word.

difficulties of the inscription) seems to be in no. 90, where Asklepias set up a stele to Men as a ransom for Diogenes. The attitude implied is clear, that the person is being held captive by the god (cf. the use of κατέχω which we will discuss below), through a disease or other punishment, and that the god must be paid to free him.[20]

In the three other inscriptions using forms of this word, the situation is somewhat complicated by the wording. In no. 57, the dedicants ἐγλυτρω[σάμεν]οι ἀνέστη[σαν] the stele. Even more peculiarly phrased are nos. 61 and 66. In no. 61 we read that the dedicants μετὰ τῶν συγγενῶν ἐξ ἰδότων καὶ μὴ ἰδότων paid their λύτρον κατ' ἐπιταγήν to the gods (Men Tyrannos, Zeus Ogmenos, etc.). This puzzling inscription has been subjected to various interpretations,[21] but in 1962 another inscription was published, our no. 66, which sheds some light on the situation. In this one we read that the dedicants ἐλυτρώσαντο τὸν θεὸν (sc. Μῆνα ἐγ Διοδότου) ἐξ εἰδότων καὶ μὴ εἰδότων. Aside from the puzzling appearance of the god in the accusative, where one rather expects ἑαυτούς or the name of another person, this inscription at least makes it clear that the phrase ἐξ ἰδότων καὶ μὴ ἰδότων cannot apply to the relatives in no. 61. The word order in no. 66 precludes that interpretation both for itself, and, by extension, for no. 61.[22] The only proper explanation,[23] however difficult it may be even in the strange Greek of this area to take ἰδότων as passive, is that we here have people paying a λύτρον to secure their release from witting and unwitting sin.[24] Thus this

[20] Steinleitner, *op. cit.*, p. 37 ff., has an extensive discussion of this concept, with many usages of the word cited, and concludes that the basic idea is that of a slave bought free from a master: the human, held in sin, is bought free and resumes his former good relations with the god. The similarity to Judeo-Christian theology does not need underlining.

As to the possibility that this inscription is not from Synaus at all (as I have it listed in *CMRDM*, I, but rather from the area of Kula, see my article in *Anatolian Studies*, 25, 1975, p. 110.

[21] E.g., ἕξ for ἐξ in Steinleitner, making six relatives; or relatives knowing or not knowing what sin had been committed. Cf. Herrmann's discussion, *op. cit.*, pp. 47-48, especially p. 47, note 182.

[22] Thus the correct interpretation does away with Steinleitner's argument, pp. 93-94, as to the transference of sin to innocent parties. But see below for instances where this argument *can* be applied to other inscriptions.

[23] As Herrmann realizes, *op. cit.*, p. 48.

[24] Parallels can be cited from Steinleitner, no. 14 — κατ' ἄγνοιαν — and

inscription is to be compared with our no. 35, discussed already, in which the dedicants do not thank the god so much for their release from sickness, as they regard it to have been the result of some misdeed on their part, which required them to propitiate the gods. The concept of ἁμαρτία is also developed in these documents, as we see from nos. 42, 70, 71, and 77.[25] The attitude of Men-worshippers would seem to be almost that of the Christian Scientists. All human suffering is caused by "error," some offense, even unconscious, against the god.[26]

No. 61 has already introduced us to another phrase common in the Lydian Men-cult and in related cults: κατ' ἐπιταγήν. It occurs in nos. 33, 49, 53, 54, 61, and 85, and with the variation ἐξ ἐπιταγῆς in the Phrygian inscription no. 93. With it can be compared the phrase ἐπέταξεν θεός in the mysterious inscription no. 76. The god can command a simple vow (nos. 33, 93), or the erection of an altar (nos. 49, 85), or a λύτρον (no. 61), or finally can compel an action on the part of a cult organization (nos. 53, 54). In the first of these two inscriptions, both apparently referring to the same event, and dated to the same month of the same year, a ἱερὸς δοῦμος (I will return to a discussion of this organization later), orders a vow to be observed after nine days to Zeus Masphalatenos, Men Tiamou, and Men Tyrannos. In the second, we have the actual vow, presumably recorded on a stele nine days later, although the organization now calls itself ἱερὰ συμβίωσις καὶ νεωτέρα, Zeus has aged remarkably, and Men Tyrannos as a separate entity has been forgotten, giving his title to Zeus, who is here called Κοίριος Τύραννος. Regrettably, exactly what the δοῦμος or συμβίωσις was doing during this period of a novena remains unexplained.[27]

---

no. 16 — ἀκουσίως. Both are from Sandal, and one describes the cutting, in ignorance, of sacred trees, and the other the involuntary breaking of a little stele. The steles here, incidentally, seem to have been susceptible to a good deal of damage. Cf. *Archäologische Zeitung*, 38, 1880, p. 38 = Berlin, *Beschreibung*, no. 681, and account of how a stele was broken by a bull and had to be replaced. And our no. 50 is an actual example of a stele both broken and repaired in antiquity.

[25] Cf. the discussion by Steinleitner, *op. cit.*, pp. 83-84, and the similar use of the word in the Sounion inscriptions, Lauffer, *op. cit.*, p. 184 (= 948).

[26] Cf. the discussion, Steinleitner, p. 99, with parallels to Christianity.

[27] As a parallel, one can adduce a passage of Aelius Aristides, Ἱεροὶ Λόγοι,

To return to the matter at hand, the phrase κατ' ἐπιταγήν. As in no. 47 we remarked that we did not know how Trophime was called by the god, likewise in these inscriptions it is left unclear how the god's command is communicated to the worshipper. I think it would be fair in this regard to cite Aelius Aristides, whose whole life was so controlled by Asclepius, and who did many things on the god's command, even being instructed as to the exact wording of a dedication.[28] In Aristides' case we know for a certainty that the god's commands were communicated by dreams. Although we do not find the phrase κατ' ὄναρ[29] anywhere in the present series of inscriptions, I do not think that it would be unreasonable to suppose that some, at least, of these commands came by dream. After all, although these people were certainly less well educated than Aristides, and their gods obviously less concerned with the niceties of wording, Aelius Aristides should still be regarded as a typical, if exaggerated, product of his age, not as an isolated phenomenon.

To see the commands as going through human mouthpieces of the gods (we will have occasion to return to this subject later also) is possible in spite of the paucity of references to cult-officials in these cults, but not as likely, it seems to me. Again, the picture we get from Aelius Aristides is that although there certainly were officials in the service of Asclepius, they did not interfere in man's direct communication with the god.[30]

Light may be shed on the subject of divine communication by

V, 42, that the god can order a fast: τὴν δὲ ἀσιτίαν ἀπέδωκα ... ἐπιταχθεῖσαν εἰς τὴν ἐπιοῦσαν. Note the similarity of vocabulary to our inscriptions.

[28] Ἱεροὶ Λόγοι, IV, 45.

[29] Cf. Herrmann's discussion of commands by dream, *op. cit.*, p. 32, note 115; the dedication by the rhetor Polemon, discussed by L. Robert, *Etudes Anatoliennes*, Paris, 1937, p. 217; further discussion, *MAMA*, V, introduction, p. xli; A. D. Nock, *JHS*, 46, 1925, p. 95 ff.; Herrmann and Polatkan, *Das Testament des Epikrates, usw.*, Österreichische Akademie der Wissenschaften, *Phil.-Hist. Klasse, Sitzungsberichte*, 265, i, 1969, commentary on no. 15; finally, the inscription from Thyateira, Robert, *op. cit.*, 130-133, revised by Merkelbach, *Zeitschrift für Papyrologie und Epigraphik*, 15, 1974, p. 208, in which the dedicant learned the truth from a priestess buried at the spot, δι' ὁράματος νυκτὸς καὶ ἡμέρας.

[30] In Herrmann, *op. cit.*, no. 25, we hear of a ἱερεύς of Artemis Anaeitis, and in no. 49, of a προφῆτις of Zeus Ariou In our no. A3, we hear of a ἱέρεια Μηνὸς Ἀξιοττηνοῦ.

our inscription no. 85. In this inscription, the altar was set up by Artemon ἐπὶ τὰ ἴχνη, on the footprints supposedly left by the god in the place where he appeared to the worshipper. We unfortunately do not know where this altar was originally located. If in a sanctuary, as seems likely, we might have evidence of temple-incubation in Men-cult. If out in the open, or on the wayside, it would recall such things as Alcmaeon's appearance to Pindar.[31]

I know of two other inscriptions of Asia Minor having to do with a god's ἴχνη. Both cases, however, differ from ours in that they record dedications of metal models of the god's footprints. In the first, from Termessos,[32] the dedication is of an altar to θεὸς ἐπήκοος ὕψιστος, and has a place on the top for a bronze (presumably) model of the god's footprint. The other, from Panamara,[33] records the dedication of golden ἴχνη, presumably to Zeus, in his sanctuary. In no case that I know of, except this one, is there an altar built on the god's footprints.[34]

Another way in which a god can communicate with man is through an angel. In no. 69 we hear of the theft of a himation from a bath-house, after the god had been called upon to prevent such things (see below for the procedure). After a time (Men is usually swifter than that) the culprit, who remains unnamed, was made by a νέμεσις to bring the clothing back and admit his guilt. Since the owner could no longer be located (? — the details remain vague) the god ordered *through an angel* that the garment be sold, and the proceeds used (?) to erect the stele in question.

Pagan angels are known from Asia Minor, and the best recent discussion of them is by L. Robert.[35] He concerns himself particu-

---

[31] *Pythia*, 8, 56 ff. In general, see Steinleitner, *op. cit.*, 80 ff. for epiphanies. Cf. also the epiphanies of the god in the Attic reliefs. One may recall that in inscription no. 130, Men is called ἐπιφανής. For this adjective, see Robert, *Hellenica*, 6, 51 and Steinleitner, pp. 15-21. If no. 85 was indeed set up by the wayside, then it would recall the dedications made by Protion at Pisidian Antioch.

[32] *TAM*, III, i, no. 32.

[33] *BCH*, 51, 1927, p. 106.

[34] The matter of a god's footprints is by no means confined to Asia Minor. For instances in the cult of the Egyptian gods, see Vidman, *SIRIS*, nos. 61, 364, 415, CE 60, CE 122, with extensive further bibliography.

[35] *Anatolia*, 3, 1958, p. 120 ff. = *Opera Minora Selecta*, I, 419 ff.

larly with a dedication from Temrek, on the territory of ancient Saittae — thus quite close to our area — to Ἄγγελος Ὅσιος καὶ Δίκαιος. L. Robert collects references to other angels — gods of emanation from a higher divinity — from Carian territory. They are all of them, however, also dedications, so this is the first time that we see a pagan angel in action. As to how exactly he appeared to the culprit, or to whoever decided that the himation was to be sold, Herrmann thinks, as we did above, of an apparition in a dream.

In an article, "Les anges du paganisme,"[36] Franz Cumont makes, *inter alia*, the following points about pagan angels: that they betray the influence of general Semitic (not exclusively Jewish) religion; that they also indicate the influence of Persian religion, whose god is so far removed from the earth that he must communicate with man through intermediaries; and that they appear frequently in neo-Platonic writings and in magical papyri, to which he gives full references.[37]

Finally, under the heading of how god communicates with man, we should mention our no. A8, in which a village established (καθιέρωσεν) Men Tyrannos and his mother through the onbreathing (κατ᾽ ἐπίπνοιαν) of Zeus Kilamenenos.[38] It is likewise left unclear

[36] *Revue de l'Histoire des Religions*, 72, 1915, pp. 159-182.

[37] This whole business of angels and other intermediate spirits between gods and man is very characteristic of the age, and too big a topic for us to begin to treat it here. For angels, cf. F. Sokolowski, *Harvard Tehological Review*, 53, 1960, 225-229, who thinks primarily of Hecate, and Hermes, in their capacity of messengers, or Thomas Kraabel, *art. cit.*, p. 83, for whom the *Sühneninschriften*, angels, and τὸ θεῖον are all aspects of a remote and unapproachable god. This hierarchy of divinity finds its reflection in a characteristic writing of this period, Apuleius' *Apologia*, particularly chap. 43. Valette, *L'Apologie d'Apulée*, Paris, 1908, has a good discussion of intermediary spirits in Antonine-period religion, p. 221 ff. Moon beliefs, of course, tie in with this, as the moon is supposed to receive the spirits of the dead awaiting purification. See Valette, *op. cit.*, p. 242, and F. Cumont's chapter "La Lune, séjour des morts," in his *Recherches sur le Symbolisme Funéraire des Romains*, Paris, 1942. Apuleius, of course, is both at least a self-styled Platonist and a man, for all his denying it, with a hefty interest in magic.

[38] For a parallel to the καθιέρωσις of a god, see the inscription from the *Koloenon katoikia*, Roscher's *Lexikon*, s.v. Sabazius, col. 243-244, and most recently Robert, *Hellenica*, 6, pp. 111-113. I argue that this inscription is probably from Kula itself, *Anatolian Studies*, 25, 1975, pp. 107-108. Cf. also the use of the same word in our no. 99, in which a dead person is dedicated to a

just how this "inspiration" which stimulated action by a whole community took place, but it seems at least to be a more gentle sort of command than an ἐπιταγή.

We have already discussed no. 47, in which the god punished an offense against himself, and no. 69, in which the god is called on preventively to keep anything from being stolen from a bath-house. This is merely a special case of the god's more general function as adjudicator of disputes among humans, and introduced us to the action, and formula, regularly used in this connection: ἐπεστάθη σκῆπτρον. It would seem that the god's involvement in human affairs is an outgrowth of his punishment of offenses against himself (nos. 47 and 80) and that he becomes involved in purely human affairs through the device of the oath — that sacrament of which ancient pagan gods are κατ' ἐξοχήν the protectors. Perjury is not merely a crime among humans, but an offense against the god. At the risk, perhaps, of being a little Procrustean in my treatment of the evidence, I would argue that it is perjury which serves the important function of getting the gods involved in affairs between humans.[39]

If we can trust the heavy restoration of no. 67, for which Keil and von Premerstein really offer little in the way of justification —

god, or Wagener, *Académie Royale de Belgique, Mémoires Couronnés*, 30, 1859, p. 19, no. 2. E. Schwertheim remarks, *Istanbuler Mitteilungen*, 25, 1975, p. 358-9, that the only parallel for the use of ἐπίπνοια (*Inschriften von Magnesia*, 100 = *SIG*³, 695) also involves a god's command to a whole community.

[39] Here I disagree with Steinleitner, *op. cit.*, pp. 100-101, who does not view the oath as the fundamental element in these cases. In my view, the role of oath in these inscriptions is rightly emphasized by Otto Eger, "Eid und Fluch in den maionischen und phrygischen Sühne-Inschriften," *Festschrift Paul Koschaker*, Weimar, 1939, III, 281 ff. He cites from the code of Justinian, 4, 1, 2, "Iurisiurandi contempta religio satis deum ultorem habet." Fear of committing perjury is proportionate to the fear of divine punishment.

Consequently Eger sharply rejects the contention of Zingerle that these cases took place before a priestly (or a human) court, and restricts the function of the priest to the ceremonies in the temple — first the σκῆπτρον or πιττάκιον, then the eventual settling of the matter.

Eger also makes the observation that, except for our no. 44, the σκῆπτρον-procedure is restricted to cases in which the other party is unknown, cases in which there is already a suspect being handled by the simple ὅρκος or πιττάκιον. Admittedly, the evidence is limited, but Eger's observation is borne out by two subsequent finds, nos. 69 and 71.

but our discussion may offer more —, the original crime about which the case at law ([ἀντιδίκων]) arose is nowhere mentioned, but the sheer fact of perjury ([ἐπιορκήσας]), is by itself considered a defilement or outrage ([λύ]μην), and is punished by the god who demands the usual writing of the case on a stele.

The oaths which involve the god in these human cases, although apparently left undescribed in no. 67, are variously described in other inscriptions. Commonest is the putting of a scepter on an altar, recorded in nos. 43, 44, 62, 69 and 71. The connection of a scepter with oaths, of course, is familiar all the way back to Homer, *e.g.*, the scene in Book I of the Iliad between Achilles and Agamemnon. Presumably this procedure was illustrated in the relief of the now lost no. 62. Other terms may be used, in addition to or instead of the scepter-formula. In no. 44, we have the phrase ἀρὰς ἔθηκεν; presumably the curses were written out and were to come down on the head of the perjurer. (Only in this case they rebounded onto the head of the perjured woman who had herself shamelessly called upon the god to support her false story!) In no. 58, we hear the phrase πιττάκιον ἔδωκεν when a man wishes vengeance for somehow having been slandered about wine.[40] It can be presumed that the tablet contained a statement of the issues involved in the case, and/or curses similar to those mentioned in no. 44, only in this case they did not come back to roost on the head of the man who called the god into play.[41] Finally we hear of oaths pure and simple (no. 51), without any paraphernalia: ὤμοσε τοὺς προγεγραμμένους θεούς and at the end ἔλοισε τοὺς ὅρκους, the last phrase getting us back into the psychological realm of λύτρον, and having to buy oneself free of guilt before the god.

Finally, in this connection, it should be observed that in nos. 43 and 44, the scepter was placed on the altar when not only had a

[40] Steinleitner, p. 100 ff., seems to me to make too much of the word πιττάκιον. For this word, cf. A. Wilhelm, *Beiträge zur griechischen Inschriftenkunde*, Vienna, 1909.

[41] Cf. the phrase λυθῆναι τὸ σκῆπτρον in no. 44. Steinleitner no. 3 = Keil and von Premerstein, *Bericht über eine Zweite Reise in Lydien*, ÖAW Denkschriften, Phil.-Hist. Klasse, 54, ii, 1911, no. 208, an inscription in which the name of the god involved is unfortunately lost, provides an illustrative parallel for the importance of oaths in these cases — in this case, one of cattle-theft.

crime been committed, but there were already (admittedly only suspects in no. 43) two distinct parties to the case ... a plaintiff and a defendant, if you will. No. 62 differs somewhat, in that a crime had been committed, but by parties completely unknown (so there could be no perjury yet) and the scepter was placed on the altar by the whole community (ἡ Ταζηνῶν κατοικία), the gods' function being here first to ferret out, and then to punish the wrongdoers. Also, as we have seen in no. 69, the procedure could be done preventively, before any crime was committed, and the same applies to no. 71, where the scepter procedure is combined in a funerary inscription with the regular appeal to the gods to protect the tomb. Thus, from the basic idea of oaths and perjury, through which the god was first involved in these human cases, the scepter procedure finds wider application among the rustic inhabitants of this area.

The cases themselves, sometimes described in detail, concern themselves with a multitude of homely occurrences. In no. 43 we have a case of wandering pigs; in no. 44, a case in which a woman was secretly giving poison to her son-in-law, causing his madness — she replied by setting the scepter on the altar against her slanderers, but it was discovered that she was rightly charged.[42] In no. 51, we have a failure to return deposited money, whereas in no. 58 we hear the unexplained slander about wine, mentioned above, and in no. 62, we have a case in which orphans were being stolen from and otherwise mistreated by moneylenders and other unknown parties ... a case which the whole community disapproved of (ἀδοξήσασα) and decided to do something about. Finally, in no. 69, we have the theft of a himation from a public bath and in the fragmentary no. 55 we may be dealing with a case of murder.

What is significant in all these cases, whether the crime was large or small, is the relative speed (no. 69 is an exception — μετὰ χρόνον) and severity of the god's punishment. As one sees in suffering the outcome of some unknown sin, so does one that much more attribute every tribulation to the punishment of god for some sin which has

---

[42] Cf. Steinleitner no. 3 = Keil and von Premerstein, *Zweite Reise*, p. 106, no. 208, already referred to above, as a parallel for our no. 43. In it the theft of animals brings about a harsh punishment, namely the death of the culprit's cattle and daughter.

become public knowledge. In the case of the swine-thief of no. 43, death was the punishment, as it was also in the case of Skollos, the cheating banker of no. 51. In both cases relatives make amends — in no. 43 only to the gods, in no. 51 to gods and men. In no. 43, Hermogenes' wife, child, and brother set up the stele; in no. 51, Skollos' daughter not only apparently repays the money but honors the gods. The vocabulary is similar to that of no. 35, discussed above, where the crime was unknown — using words like "propitiated" (ἱλάσαντο no. 43; εἱλασαμένη no. 51[43]) and "blessing" (εὐλογοῦμεν no. 43; εὐλογεῖ no. 51) the gods for their powers (δυνάμις).[44] No. 44 shows that the punishment could be spread to other members of the family.[45] Not only did Tatias, the wicked mother-in-law, suffer an unspecified punishment (οἱ θεοὶ αὐτὴν ἐποίησαν ἐ[ν] κολάσει ἣν οὐ διέφυγεν) but her son Sokrates — here the situation is described in great detail if sketchy grammar — while going through the entrance that led into the grove, dropped a vinecutting sickle on his foot, thus causing his death (?) — at any rate a swift and horrible sounding punishment awaited him (μονημέρῳ κολάσει ἀπηλλάγη). (One may well wonder, however, reading between the lines of this inscription, whether Tatias was not in fact innocent, and the whole interpretation made up to suit the events which did in actuality ensue. Certainly, it would require a great deal of temerity to forswear oneself by a god known for such efficacious punishments.) Again relatives, consisting of or at least including, paradoxically enough, the children of the intended poisoning victim, must make amends.

We have the usual vocabulary — ἐξειλασάμενοι ... εὐλογοῦμεν στηλλογραφήσαντες τὰς δυνάμις.[46] In no. 62, the case of the orphans being mistreated, the punishment is left undefined (ὁ θεὸς ἐξεζήτησεν

---

[43] For this word, see Robert, *Hellenica*, 6, p. 108.

[44] Cf. also the use of ὁμολογῶ in the Sardis inscription no. 77, as contrasted with the negated forms of the same verb in no. 43. Cf. also the use of εὐείλατος in the Sounion inscriptions, which, as we have already seen, have several points of coincidence in wording with the Lydian material.

[45] Thus backing up Steinleitner's idea, *op. cit.*, pp. 93-94, but with material unknown to him.

[46] Cf. Steinleitner, *op. cit.*, p. 78, who contrasts the thankfulness of the votive inscriptions with the tenor of these last discussed documents, and on p. 80 compares Plutarch, *De Superstitione*, VII, 168C.

[καὶ] ἐκολάσετο τοὺς [ἐπι]βουλεύσαντας). But familiar words reappear — ἐστηλλογράφησαν [τὰ]ς δυνάμις. Only in no. 50, to repeat, do we see a compassionate and forgiving god.

From these inscriptions, I think that it is clear what an important role Men and the divinities associated with him played in the life of the common people of this area. This role is not only important, but threatening and powerful. It should thus come as no surprise that the god is frequently thought of as a supreme ruler (βασιλεύων) or possessor, occupier of a certain place (κατέχων).[47]

I do not think that it is really necessary with Buckler[48] to see the proceedings of our no. 51 as taking place in a secular law-court. Much less is it necessary with Zingerle[49] to see an elaborate system of priestly tribunals.[50] Not only are the mentions of priests in this cult scarce, but one would have to assume that we are here dealing with temple-estates which had become imperial estates, but in which the temples kept secular jurisdiction. This was a theory held by some of the older scholars, such as Ramsay and Rostovzeff, but it has lost ground in view of more recent discoveries. In particular there is no evidence of temple estates around here unless these inscriptions be taken as such — a circular argument.[51] Rather the procedure is to be seen as happening without, or with a minimum of human intervention. Except for no. 67, where the legal terminology might seem to refer to preceding action in a civil court, there is no more need to see human, specifically priestly, intervention than in our discussion of κατ' ἐπιταγήν or δι' ἀνγέλου. The parties of the dispute — we may imagine — go to the temple and make their

[47] Compare the phrase φιλάνθρωπον πολυάρητον βασιλῆα used of Men in no. 126. Cf. also the epithets τύραννος and κύριος. The matter is discussed by Steinleitner, op. cit., p. 77, although the latter epithet is attested for Men from Lydia only indirectly in no. 43. See also Bömer, op. cit., p. 203 (= 405) ff., who, however, continues to follow the old reasoning of temple estates, etc.
[48] ABSA, 21, 1914-16, p. 179.
[49] Österreichische Jahreshefte, 23, 1926, Beiblatt, col. 29 ff.
[50] Steinleitner, op. cit., p. 108, seems to be on the right track in seeing all this as happening automatically. On p. 105 he sees rightly that the inscriptions have no hint of real litigation, but even he, p. 111, ascribes what I consider an exaggerated importance to the priesthood. See also the resumé of Eger's article in note 39, above.
[51] See T. R. S. Broughton in Studies in Honor of A. C. Johnson, Princeton, 1951, p. 236 ff.

statements in view of the gods whom all of them respect and fear. What happens after that happens by itself, until the smitten parties or their remaining relatives go again to the temple to record the gods' powers. The words κατέχων or βασιλεύων are likewise not to be taken as denoting literal political suzerainty of the gods in these areas, but rather the hold that they had over the minds of the people.

In nos. 51 and 67, both heavily restored inscriptions, it would appear that Men is simply said to be τὴν κώμην βασιλεύων although probably in no. 51 there was space for some further geographical precision to be added. However, in all these inscriptions, where the relevant portion is actually preserved, Men, with or without other gods, is said to be ruling a specific place. In nos. 43, 86, and A1 it is Ἄξιττα (Ἀξίοττα) and, the same name is to be read in no. 44 — μεγάλοι οὖν οἱ θεοὶ οἱ ἐν Ἀξίττοις. Since nos. 43 and 44 were found presumably in Ayazviran, and no. A1 in Menye, whereas the provenience of no. 86 is not definitely known, it is impossible to equate the name with any specific known present day locality.[52] Further, it is obvious that the place-name is connected with the widespread epithet Ἀξιοττηνός[53]. I would like therefore to suggest that the name Ἄξιττα does not belong to a specific place, at least not in the normal sense of the word, but is a hieratic, non-secular name applying to this whole area. Support can be found for this view, I think, in nos. 162 and 163, from Antioch in Pisidia, which speak of Men as having charge over (ναέτης, μεδέων) an area Ἀσκαίη. Like Ἄξιττα, this place name is connected with a widespread epithet, Ἀσκαηνός, not only standard at Antioch, but found at a number of Phrygian and Carian sites, and on the coins of Sardis.[54] Here it is clear that

---

[52] Unlike Herrmann and Polatkan, *Das Testament des Epikrates*, pp. 39-41, I do not think one should even particularly try to localize the name. They are, however, on a better track when they speculate that Axitta may have been an alternate name for Maionia, "besonders auf den lokal-kultischen Bereich beschränkt."

[53] Found not only on monuments of this immediate area, nos. 31, 32, 33, 38, 42, 47, 48, 50, 58, 68, 70, 71, 72, A2, A3, but of Sardis, nos. 77, 80, and on coins of the nearby Saittae, nos. 4-6. The name has a striking resemblance to those of the gods worshipped in the Samothracian mysteries, but this may be mere coincidence.

[54] Monuments nos. 87, 101, 105, 106, 107, 118, 119, 120, 130, 131 and Sardis coins nos. 1-4.

the name must be connected with the Ἀσκανία Λίμνη (= Lake of Iznik and Lake of Burdur), with Vergil's Ascanius, and with the Ἀσκανίη of Homer,[55] and thus have a vague reference to all of Asia Minor, not to one specific place.[56]

Remarkable also are the more specific names of places which Men is supposed to govern, and, since these names likewise are not attested elsewhere, one may well ask whether they too in some cases may not be the sacred names of the places, not used in normal secular language.

In no. 42, the place governed is apparently Δόρου κώμη. This place may have something to do with the Δορηνοί of an inscription copied by Buresch.[57] A parallel for the genitive of a person's name and the word κώμη is furnished, on the most likely interpretation, by the Ἀρχελάου κώμη of no. A8. I do not find the exact name Δόρος recorded anywhere, the closest being Δῶρος, the name of the mythical ancestor of the Dorians.[58]

In no. 47, the place is called Κόρεσα. I cannot claim certainty, but I think that this is a real place too, probably to be identified with the modern village of Köres.[59]

No. 69 gives us Men ruling Τάρσι, which, since the exact findspot of this inscription is unknown, following Herrmann,[60] I tended in *CMRDM*, I, to locate at the village of Köleköy. I am now, however, of the opinion that this is another hieratic name, probably, like Ἀσκαίη, intended to stand for all of Asia Minor, rather than a specific place.[61] Furthermore, there exists the possibility that this name too, through real or imagined connections with the Etruscans, was supposed to link Men and other divinities, such as Apollo Tarsios and Mother Tarsene, to Italy, raising the possibility of

---

[55] *Iliad*, B, 863; N 793.

[56] On possible propaganda value extracted from this by the Romans, see my article in *Numen*, 22, 1975, pp. 235-236.

[57] *Aus Lydien*, Leipzig, 1898, p. 77, no. 38; cf. Keil and von Premerstein, *Zweite Reise*, p. 92 ff.

[58] Cf. Pape-Benseler, *Wörterbuch der griechischen Eigennamen, s.v.* See also below, Ch. 6, n. 20.

[59] See my article, "Two Notes on Lydian Topography," *Anatolian Studies*, 25, 1975.

[60] *Op. cit.*, p. 34.

[61] See my article, "The Italian Connection," *Numen*, 22, 1975, pp. 235-239.

deliberate fostering of the cult by the Roman authorities, and offering some explanation for the mysterious Μήν Ἰταλικός of our no. 93.

Another interesting aspect of the Men-cult in Lydia is provided by the various groups that worshipped him. The most striking is the ἱερὸς δοῦμος of no. 53. The name of this cult-organization is seemingly glossed in no. 54 (the paying of the vow made nine days before) by ἱερὰ συμβίωσις[62] καὶ νεωτέρα, perhaps assuming that it would be better this time to use a more generally comprehensible word. The word is rare indeed, and would seem to refer to a kind of cult-community. In an inscription of the same area,[63] dated 223-224 A.D., we hear of a δοῦμος that honors Aurelius Glycon, priest of Artemis Anaeitis, for his "religion to the gods" (τὴν ἰς τοὺς θεοὺς θρησκείαν), and his many services to the *doumos*. The chances are strong[64] that we are dealing with the exact same organization, which has endured some fifty years.

The other references to the word, including some that are quite speculative, have been gathered by S. Wikander,[65] who follows L. Deubner in the explanation of the unusual Latin word *dumopireti* as being from δοῦμος and πύραιθοι, betraying Zoroastrian and Iranian influence. The major examples cited by Wikander are:

1. Our inscription D3, but the other side than that which has been connected with Men-cult.

2. An epigram of Philodemus of Gadara,[66] bristling with obscure words, but ostensibly the epitaph of a worshipper of the Mother of the Gods, one Trygonion, ᾗ καλύβη καὶ δοῦμος ἐνέπρεπεν, "in whom the hut (chapel) and the *doumos* were outstanding."[67]

---

[62] Note the use of συμβίωσις φιλία in the cult of Sarapis, Vidman, *SIRIS*, 154 = *IG*, XII, 5, 192 (Tenos). For other uses of συμβίωσις in Lydia, see Buresch, *op. cit.*, p. 54-55, with references to Artemidorus (himself a Lydian) as to the activities of these groups. See also L. Robert, *Etudes Anatoliennes*, 63 ff., and *Hellenica*, 9, 1950, p. 35.

[63] Herrmann, *op. cit.*, no. 25.

[64] Herrmann, p. 38.

[65] *Feuerpriester in Kleinasien und Iran*, Lund, 1946, p. 2 ff.

[66] *Anthologia Palatina*, VII, 222.

[67] Note, however, that our Lydian *doumos*, unlike the one from Serdica, contained no women. Most editors before Buresch, incidentally, emended to δοῦπος. Cf. the commentary on this poem by Gow and Page, *The Garland of*

3. An inscription discovered by Buresch on Mt. Toma in Lydia, north of the Hermus:[68]

172-3 A.D. Ἔτους σνζ΄, μη(νὸς) Ἀρτεμισί[ου]
γι΄ ἀνεστάθη ὁ βωμὸς προνο[ήσαν-]
τος τοῦ δούμου ἐκ τῶν ἰδίων
τῆς ναυκόρου.

This is the only one really relevant for our purposes. It is perhaps the same organization, in spite of some geographical distance, and it is only one year later than the inscriptions regarding the nine-day vow. The connection with temple personnel is there again, as in the inscription in which the *doumos* honors the priest of Anaeitis, even if the exact relationship is unclear.[69]

Even more mysterious than the *doumos* are the καταλουστικοί mentioned in inscriptions 34 and A3, separated in time only two years. The geographical distance between findspots is not great, and whereas these people are said to be worshippers of three gods in no. 34, they are not attributed to any god in no. A3, although they honor a priestess of Men Axiottenos. It is therefore possible, I think, that we are dealing with the same organization, which, unlike our *doumos*, contains both men and women. The real question is exactly what these καταλουστικοί did that gave them their name. Keil and von Premerstein[70] think of some kind of ritual purification, undertaken in the course of a mystery cult. But since mysteries in the cult of Men are hardly attested (cf. no. 75, to be discussed below), it would seem more likely to associate them with the non-mystic purifications before worship specified in the Xanthus-inscriptions

Philip, II, Cambridge, 1968, p. 396 ff., for other conjectures involving the word δοῦμος.

[68] *Op. cit.*, p. 58 ff.

[69] Apart from this, Buresch's interpretation seems grammatically forced and unlikely, although he may be on to something in that part of his argumentation which notes the resemblance of "Lydian" terms to Greek and Latin ones. For instance, he notes the resemblance of δοῦμος to *domus*, etc., "house." However, he takes all these connections to be real, rather than as merely supposed, as we do. What he says about prietesses with mother goddesses and priests with male divinities simply does not hold water in the light of subsequent discoveries.

[70] *Zweite Reise*, p. 95. Cf. Bömer, *op. cit.*, p. 206 (= 488) on the importance of the long lists of names with these dedications.

of Attica, the similarities of which to the Lydian material we have already had occasion to comment upon.[71] Still, we cannot really be sure about the function of these people until more information becomes available.

Another mysterious group appears in our no. 57, admittedly a corrupt text, οἱ συμβολαφόροι. Here, however, we are on safe ground, it seems to me, drawing on parallels from elsewhere within the cult of Men itself. Our no. 75, an inscription from another part of Lydia than that discussed hitherto, far to the S.W. and over Mt. Tmolus from the area that we have been dealing with, speaks of a dedication to Men, described as προκαθήμενος τῆς κώμης (a milder form, perhaps, of the κατέχων or βασιλεύων that we discussed above) of a σημήαν περιάργυρον τὴν προπομπεύουσαν τῶν μυστηρίων αὐτοῦ. The nature of this silver-bordered standard, perhaps containing a likeness of the god, as well as similar phenomena in other moon-cults, such as that of Sin at Carrhae, have been discussed at length by H. W. Pleket.[72] What is clear from this inscription is that there were sacred processions in honor of Men, in which images of the god or symbols can be imagined to have been carried around. (Not that we can jump to the conclusion, however, that there must have been mysteries of Men in the area of Kula — that remains a peculiarity of no. 75.) Further, from our no. 57 it appears that the carriers of symbols formed a special group of some sort in the service of the god. Now, of course, the question arises, why should these people, who perform a special function in the god's service, together with the three individuals mentioned specifically (or so J. and L. Robert interpret it[73]) describe themselves as ἐγλυτρωσάμενοι, assuming that Herrmann's restoration is right? It does not seem too far-fetched to suggest that we are dealing here with another inscription of the "offense-against-the-god" category. It would appear that in the course of the procession something went wrong or was done in an unseemly manner by the persons named, that they thus found themselves in disfavor

---

[71] Cf. such phrases as λουσάμενοι κατακέφαλα. Keil and von Premerstein perceive the similarity also.

[72] *Mnemosyne*, Ser. 4, 23, 1970, pp. 192-195; *Talanta*, 2, 1970, 55-82. This latter article also has a very good discussion of the word προκαθήμενος, and gives *Almoura* as the ancient name of the place the inscription was found.

[73] *REG*, 26, 1963, p. 167, no. 225.

with the god, and had to buy themselves free by the confession of their fault and the erection of this stele.

We have already had occasion to mention that the role of the priests in Men-cult seems to be surprisingly small, at least in this area. This is not to say that they do not exist. We hear, however, of only one specifically, and that is a *priestess*, honored by the καταλουστικοί in our no. A3. It is instructive to compare this inscription with one published by Peter Herrmann,[74] in which a *doumos* honors a priest of Artemis Anaeitis, as the reasons for honoring seem to be much the same. The priest of Anaeitis is honored διὰ τὴν ἰς τοὺς θεοὺς θρησκείαν and τὰς ἰς τὸν δοῦμον πολλὰς εὐεργησίας and the priestess of Men Axiottenos for τὴν ἰς [τοὺς] θεοὺς εὐσέβειαν καὶ θρησκείαν and τὴν πρὸς πάντας ἀνθρώπους φιλοκἀγαθίαν.

That is to say, for piety (religiosity?) towards the gods in general,[75] and for benefactions and kindliness to men, either specifically the cult-organization, or all men in general. To this there is added in A3 the fact that the priestess of Men had consorted with the god without desire for profit — ἀναστραφεῖσαν ἐπὶ τῷ θεῷ ἀφιλοκέρδως. The assumption is that it might have been possible for her to make some profit out of her position, but she refused to do so.[76] In both cases the priesthood seems to be hereditary. The inscription honoring the priest of Artemis Anaeitis uses the phrase τῆς συγγενικῆς θεοῦ and mentions the honorand's son and grandson; the one honoring the priestess of Men uses the phrase διὰ γένους. In the case of the priestess, at least, the tenure is for life (παντὶ τῷ βίῳ). Furthermore the temple of Buresch's inscription from Mt. Toma, which he assumes to have been dedicated to a mother goddess, had a female

---

[74] *Op. cit.*, no. 25.

[75] Θρησκεία is used here not as a specific cult, as, *e.g.*, in Herrmann and Polatkan, *op. cit.*, no. 1, line 51, but virtually as a synonym for εὐσέβεια. For the development of this word see, L. Robert, *Etudes Anatoliennes*, p. 28 and p. 517.

[76] We simply do not know enough about the finances of these rural sanctuaries to know how she might have been expected *to* make a profit out of her position. The fact that she did *not* do so, however, testifies to the fact that Men-cult in this area, at least, did not try to enrich itself at the expense of the worshippers. This is to be contrasted with the Men-temple of no. 121, and the fact that the Men-priests of central Asia Minor seem to have been local nabobs.

ναυκόρος who on the likeliest interpretation gave the money for the *doumos* to dedicate an altar. This, too, is a benefaction to the *doumos*.

Nowhere, however, do we find the slightest hint of the priest serving as a real intermediary between god and man, such as some scholars have attempted to see in cases where one "asks the god" something, or in the quasi-judicial inscriptions. All that still seems to happen by itself, in a direct relationship between worshipper and deity. The priest's role still seems to be very restricted, and his functions, perhaps, purely ceremonial.[77]

A last word is necessary about a cult-gesture with which the worshippers of Men express their recognition of the god's powers. This is the gesture of the upraised hand. This gesture, found also on the Attic reliefs nos. 2 and 10, in which the worshippers hail Men on animal-back, occurs in nos. 39, 60, 63, 69, and A2. Except in the case of 69, the gesture is made with the right hand alone, and seems to be associated with the beneficent workings of the god, his showing his power to heal. Only in no. 69, the account of the theft of the himation from the bath-house, is there a variation. The small figure in the separate panel presumably represents the culprit, found out, although belatedly, by divine justice, and acknowledging his fault by raising both hands over his head.

---

[77] The only exception to this picture, in the whole area, is the προφῆτις of Zeus Ariou in Herrmann, *op. cit.*, no. 49, who is credited with the σωτηρία of the dedicant. This inscription, with its possible reference to an oracular cult (known in connection with Men only from no. 129) would seem to offer the only known support from inscription of this area to the theory of Steinleitner and others, in which cult-personnel play an important role.

For other priesthoods of the area, either of non-related or of unspecified gods, some held only for limited periods, see Herrmann, nos. 10, 16, and 28.

CHAPTER THREE

THE CULT IN ASIA MINOR, APART FROM LYDIA AND ANTIOCH IN PISIDIA

It is a little hard trying to put together a chapter on this subject because of the sheer disparity of the material. Unlike the relative masses of material from the cult centers, the material from the other areas of Asia Minor, perhaps because it was so originally, perhaps because of less thorough exploration and discovery, is more scattered and does not fit so nicely into patterns.

One thing that does, however, seem to characterize the "Phrygian" material — Phrygian is such a vague geographical term as to be almost meaningless — is vows on behalf of whole communities. If we observed in the Lydian material that Men sometimes was κατέχων or βασιλεύων a given place, and once that a whole community, the Ταζηνῶν κατοικία, appealed to him, so in a number of cases from Northern Phrygia (nos. 88, 93, 97, 98, 105, and 108) he is called on for the safety of a whole group or community. Often this appeal is connected with the idea of σωτηρία. Usually little, if anything, is known about these communities, except what can be gathered from these very inscriptions, and perhaps from a few others.

The first is from the Ἀλιανῶν κατοικία. Since the location of the finding of the stone seems to be known, and since the numismatically attested city of Alia seems to be located elsewhere, we must distinguish between the two places.[1]

No. 93 is an inscription of the area of Eskişehir, and records a vow of the Οὐεζαεῖται, ἐξ ἐπιταγῆς (i.e., the god could order a vow by a whole community as in no. A8). This ethnic is also known from an inscription of the nearby village of Avdan,[2] a vow to Zeus Bronton by two individuals on behalf of their families and the Οὐεζαεῖται.

---

[1] See Drexler, in Roscher's *Lexikon*, s.v. Men, col. 2709; Reinach, *REG*, 3, 1890, p. 52. I have discussed this matter in *Anatolian Studies*, 25, 1975, 105, note 3.
[2] *MAMA*, V, 127.

No. 97 cannot be relied on too heavily, as the reading is extremely uncertain, but would seem to be a dedication to Men and Zeus Benneus by a group calling itself the Κωμηνοί. No. 98 records a vow to Men by the ’Αεζηνοί ἐνχώριοι. Since both 97 and 98 were found at Nacoleia, the original editors take them to be dedications by the inhabitants of surrounding villages.[3]

No. 105 is a dedication by an individual on behalf of a whole community — ὑπὲρ δήμου ’Απολληνῶν σωτηρίας. This would seem to be the only record of this place-name, and the basis for its identification with modern Çoğu.[4]

No. 108 is a dedication, apparently, of the δῆμος Σελμεηνῶν to Men, and this same ethnic also appears twice as an epithet of Men (nos. 107 and 109) in the same locality, thus giving a fairly certain name to the ancient site.[5] We do not seem to be dealing, as we were in Lydia, with epithets or place-names not used in normal secular language.

Similar to worship of Men on behalf of or by whole communities, is the worship of him by a φράτρα, for which we have evidence in nos. 87 and 127. We have seen already various associations in the service of Men, in Lydia and Rhodes, but the term φράτρα seems to occur only in these two inscriptions of central Asia Minor.[6] Unfortunately, neither of these inscriptions is particularly informative, although no. 87 is nicely dated to A.D. 169-170, the one φράτρα being qualified by two (?) proper names in the genitive, the other with a name in the accusative. The only thing that stands out is that one or more persons had a strong position of leadership in these organizations.

The concept of σωτηρία is peculiarly strong in the Men-inscriptions of this area. This, of course, is a common enough concept in ancient religion, usually restricting itself (as in Aelius Aristides) to

---

[3] *MAMA*, V, p. 100; the word ἐνχώριοι is discussed, *ibid.*, p. 105, and the idea advanced that it simply means "villagers."
[4] *MAMA*, I, p. xxviii.
[5] *MAMA*, VII, p. xx.
[6] For a thorough discussion of φράτρα as a title of a cult-organization, and its relation to συμβίωσις see Buresch, *Aus Lydien*, p. 130 ff. Its leader is called ἀγωνοθέτης. See also P. Herrmann, *Anz. Akad. Wien, Ph.-Hist. Klasse*, 107, 1970, p. 103; H. W. Pleket, *Talanta*, 2, 1970, p. 74.

salvation from some illness or other physical danger, and without the broader implications which the word takes on in Christianity.[7]

Whereas in the abundant Lydian material, the idea of saving crops up only in nos. 41 and 72, in the more scattered "Phrygian" material, and in that from elsewhere in central Asia Minor, it crops up in nos. 88, 91, 92, 105, 107, 142, and A6. Two of these (nos. 88 and 105) we have already had occasion to mention (no. 88 is nicely dated 190-191 A.D.) as prayers by individuals for the salvation of whole communities; nos. 91 and 92, both from the area of Eskişehir, are for the σωτηρία of family members — ὑπὲρ τέκνων σωτηρίας, περὶ τῶν ἰδίων σωτηρίας — and no. 107, from Selmea, is on behalf of the dedicant's own salvation. No. A6, an inscription from Comana in Cappadocia, and therefore far removed from any area where Men-cult had been attested prior to its discovery, is by a νεωκόρος on behalf of the σωτηρία of a priest. It is not explicitly stated whether both functionaries were in the service of Men, or the vow simply made to Men, but since no other divinity is mentioned, the likely assumption is that we are here dealing with a priest of Men and his assistant.

Finally in this regard we have the remarkable relief no. 142, of uncertain provenience, whose relief we will analyze under the heading of iconography. It bears the inscription Μηνὶ Σωτῆρι καὶ Πλουτοδώτηι. It is interesting that the same formula also occurs in Sarapis-cult, a cult with which Men-cult has much in common, both being deliberately state-sponsored cults which nonetheless caught on among the populace. (For the large number of times that this monument has been reproduced photographically, it seems remarkable that this observation has apparently never been made.) Vidman[8] republishes a syncretistic dedication discovered ca. 1912 in the Mithraeum of the Baths of Caracalla, which he dates to the time of that emperor. It has the following inscription:

Διὶ
Ἡλίῳ

---

[7] The idea is discussed by W. M. Ramsay, *The Bearing of Recent Discoveries on the Trustworthiness of the New Testament*, London, 1920, pp. 178-190, but with a paucity of examples.

[8] *SIRIS*, no. 389.

μεγάλῳ
Σαράπιδι
σωτῆρι
πλουτοδότῃ
ἐπηκόῳ
εὐεργέτῃ
ἀνεικήτῳ
Μίθρα
χαριστήριον.[9]

To my knowledge, no one has previously commented on the connection between these two inscriptions. The combination of epithets Σωτήρ Πλουτοδότης occurs nowhere else in Sarapis-cult — as a matter of fact Πλουτοδότης occurs only here — and the same can be said for no. 142 within the context of Men-cult.[10] Striking also is the fact that in our no. 142, Men has undergone a solar syncretism, the same as happens with Sarapis in the inscription which we are using as a parallel.[11] No. 142 is in many ways an anomalous monument, and the radiate crown attests to an importance of syncretism which amounts to a lack of understanding of Men's fundamentally lunar nature, in spite of all the crescents which dot the relief. Likewise, the all-embracing syncretism of the various attributes on no. 142 is generally foreign to Men-cult, although, as we shall see, most of them are explicable individually.[12]

---

[9] Vidman takes Μίθρα as nominative, a person's name. To me, however, this seems unlikely, but I confess I am unable to suggest a better interpretation.

[10] Ἐπήκοος and ἀνείκητος both are likewise attested as epithets for Men and will be discussed below in the chapter on epithets.

[11] This is common enough in Sarapis-cult. Cf. Vidman's index, p. 343, s.v. Ζεὺς Ἥλιος μέγας Σάραπις. This syncretism is not exclusively western, either, but is attested in Asia Minor and other parts of the east.

[12] Perhaps it is not too far-fetched to think that this Sarapis-inscription, as well as giving us a parallel for the wording, may also shed some light on the intellectual milieu which produced the remarkable stone, and an Italian origin for no. 142 can tentatively be suggested. After all, the only other inscriptions which show such a wide-ranging syncretism for Men are the Italian Attis-Menotyrannus inscriptions. Unfortunately, nothing whatever is known about the provenience of this piece, just as nothing is known about its present whereabouts.

The fact that priesthoods and temples of Men are best known from this area speaks for the public character of his worship in central Asia Minor, and agrees with the idea that we get from inscriptions on behalf of whole communities. There seems to be a subtle shift of emphasis between the Lydian worship, particularly the Maeonian, and that in other parts of Asia Minor, gradually leading over to the most public, state-sponsored Men-worship of all, that of Antioch in Pisidia, which so to speak stands at the other pole from the Lydian cult in several regards.

The Maeonian cult seems to have been carried on primarily in rustic sanctuaries, without elaborate personnel. For all the abundance of material, we hear of only one priestess (no. A3), and only once is a temple mentioned (no. 44). Nor does the material of this area find much reflection in the coinage — a sure sign of official sanction. The Men-coinage of Maeonia itself is sparse and early (two issues of the time of Nero), and only the city of Saittae, lying on the edge of the area in question, has a relatively abundant Men-coinage.[13]

Although Men may be called κατέχων or βασιλεύων, this is in a spiritual sense, and I think that it is significant that nowhere in the Maeonian material is there an epithet which we can identify with any known political entity, as we can Σελμεηνός.

A way-station from this unofficial and rustic cult to the more formal and official cult seems to be found at Sardis, where the inscriptions conform to the psychology of the Maeonian inscriptions, but a temple is known to have existed and to have been a recognizable landmark of the city (no. 79), and Men Askaenos is a regular divinity honored by the city on its coins, particularly in conjunction with the empresses of the first half of the third century A.D. (The empress/Men combination seems to have been the token of a certain denomination of the coinage.)

When, however, we turn to the rest of Asia Minor, where the epigraphy is scarcer, or even non-existent, and we have in some

[13] There is, in general, a discrepancy between what we know of Men-cult from the inscriptions and what we know from the coins. What we know from the literary evidence is still different. Only rarely, as at Antioch in Pisidia, do they coincide and confirm each other. We will have several occasions to observe this fact as we go ahead with this study.

cases only the numismatic evidence to go on, we find a surprisingly different picture as to temples and priesthoods.

Temples are specifically recorded or can be assumed to have existed in the following places: 1) Nysa ad Maeandrum — coins 13, 18, 30; 2) Julia — coin 4; 3) Prostanna — coins 1, 2, 3; 4) Galatia — coins 7, 8; 5) Büyük Beşkavak — monument no. 111; 6) Burdur — mon. 121; 7) Fassılar — mon. 144 (most conveniently discussed later, among the Lycaonian grave-inscriptions); 8) Apollonia Pisidiae — mon. 130; 9) Sillyon — coins 53, 54. A temple would also seem to be implied in mon. A7, from near Nicomedeia, as the place where the altar was given to Men.

Priesthoods are recorded in the following places: 1) Eumeneia — mon. 101; 2) Aphrodisias — mon. nos. 118, 119, 120; 3) Andeda — mon. 129; 4) Anaboura — mon. 131; 5) Comana Cappadociae — mon. A6 (already discussed above); 6) Ormeleis — mon. 103.

All in all then, although there is much disparity among the individual cases, it is a remarkable fact that so many temples and priesthoods should be known from areas where the material concerning Men is highly scattered. Let us examine the cases one by one:

In the case of Nysa the cult of Men is recorded only from coins. Nysa has a total of over forty coin-types which portray Men, from the time of Nero as Caesar to that of Gallienus, including two or three which show him in a temple.[14] Men's importance in Nysa is further underlined by the fact that he can appear on alliance coins with Ephesus and Sparta as the representative of the city (nos. 41, 42, and 43), and on a number of coins he is associated with the Tyche of the city.[15] Men also bears, on a number of coins of Nysa (nos. 4, 5, and 6 (?)), the epithet Καμαρείτης, only twice attested elsewhere.[16] Finally, from Nysa we have the remarkable coin of Men in the pose of a river-god (no. 29), which probably bespeaks his

[14] No. 13, Marcus Aurelius; no. 18, Elagabalus; no. 30 (?), the two Philips. The temple is, incidentally, shown on different coins in entirely different ways, so that no architectural conclusions can be drawn.
[15] Nos. 19, 21 (?), 22, 35, 36, and 40. This association of Men with Tyche is to be compared with the role Men plays elsewhere as *poliouchos*, such as at Ancyra.
[16] Monument 56; unpublished inscription known to L. Robert (see *CMRDM*, II, p. 175).

importance to the irrigation of the area and as protector against floods. (This will be discussed in greater detail under the heading of iconography.) All in all, then, considering the unique importance of Men at Nysa, it is remarkable that so far as I can determine, no epigraphical evidence for his cult there has yet been discovered. It is, however, not a unique situation.

In the case of Julia, we have a coincidence of numismatic and epigraphical evidence. Not only is there a coin of the reign of Aemilian with a representation of Men in a temple, but there are a number of inscriptions and other monuments, nos. 112-117, now in the Afyon Museum, said to have been found in the area of Julia. Unfortunately, neither are the inscriptions very informative (except that no. 115 brings us an otherwise unattested epithet for Men), nor are the museum officials of Afyon particularly willing to divulge information. It may possibly, however, be safe to assume, that these dedications are actually from the temple illustrated on our coin Julia 4.

Prostanna has three coins which represent Men, from the times of Septimius Severus, Philip the Arab, and Valerian. All show him in a temple so peculiar in decoration, however one interprets the representation, that there can be little doubt but that an actual temple and actual cult-image are being represented. But here, as in the case of Nysa, no discovery of epigraphical evidence has yet been made to confirm the numismatic evidence.

Monument no. 111, from Büyük Beşkavak — dated 89-90 A.D. — speaks of a dedication of a temple by one Lucius Sergius Korinthos. The ancient name of the site is unknown, but the editors of the inscription speculate[17] that it may lie behind the unfortunately incompletely preserved epithet of Men. They also speculate that the dedicant was a freedman of the Sergii Paulli, known to have held property in the area. At all events, I think we can safely say that we are probably dealing here with a small rural sanctuary of some sort, similar to those of Lydia, if a freedman who never left the area to seek his fortune elsewhere (so far as we know) had the funds to construct it.

[17] *MAMA*, VII, p. xxv.

Two coins of the *koinon* of the Galatians, centered in Ancyra (nos. 7, 8, both of the reign of Trajan), show Men standing in a temple, and, in general, Men is a favorite god both of the *koinon* and of the city of Ancyra, appearing on the coins of the latter from the time of Titus to that of Gallienus and Salonina, and being entrusted with the anchor, the symbol of the city, on two coins (nos. 3 and 5). Monumental evidence is also known from the same area (nos. 158-159), but the exact provenience is unsure, and neither monument has any writing.[18]

No. 121 is doubly interesting, in that it records both a cult-official (πάρεδρος) and a temple of Men, and goes into great detail about the equipment given to Men by this official. Unfortunately, a great deal of this inscription is also missing, and there is some uncertainty as to how it should be restored. Even so, it probably furnishes us more detailed information about a shrine of Men than any other inscription except those from Sounion.[19]

The offerings consist of two beds with their equipment (i.e., mattresses, pillows, etc.), and two tables. These as the Roberts observe, serve as equipment for a banquet, "whether the banqueters are divinities, priests, or worshippers."[20] If a parallel can be drawn from the ἔρανος of the second Sounion inscription, then the banqueters are mortals, although the god may figuratively be asked to join in. Next are four ἀνακλιτήρια. The Roberts conclude[21] that this word refers to easy chairs. The word is thus regularly used in Modern Greek, although the Roberts nowhere indicate this. Therefore Bean's interpretation as "benches" is less likely.[22]

---

[18] For the old theory that Men is identified with the emperor on the coin which we call, "Uncertain, perhaps Ancyra," and the fact that I consider it fanciful, see *Berytus*, 17, 1967, pp. 42-44, and *Numen*, 22, 1975, p. 239, note 21.

[19] In general, for this inscription, I refer the reader to the bibliography given in *CMRDM*, I. The Roberts originally wanted to restore the title νεωκόρος in the first line, but themselves gave up the idea in subsequent publications. G. E. Bean furnishes parallels, from Lesbos, Lycia, and Magnesia ad Maeandrum, for the word πάρεδρος being used for a subordinate priesthood, *JHS*, 42, 1952, p. 118.

[20] *Hellenica*, 9, p. 44.

[21] *Op. cit.*, pp. 45-46.

[22] In general, I feel it would be worthwhile for scholars to show more acquaintance with the present-day Greek vernacular, as present meanings often shed light on the popular language of the Imperial Period, and obviate

There is doubt as to the beginning of line 6. Robert reads [τὰ ἐν τῷ] πε[ρ]ιβόλῳ whereas Bean reads [σὺν καὶ τῷ] πε[ρ]ιβόλῳ assuming the *peribolos* not to be the whole sacred enclosure, but rather an exedra around his presumed benches. Certainty is impossible, but I lean towards Robert's restoration, which does not seem to be redundant, as Bean claims it is.[23]

In line 8, we hear of a [θυ]ρὶς καγκελλωτὴ ἐποῦσα τῷ ταμίῳ, i.e., a grilled window opening on the place that the money was kept. We seem almost to be more in the world of banking or business than in that of religion, and one can virtually see a cashier sitting behind the window described. Robert is able to cite, however, two parallels to this sort of practice in religious contexts, from Egypt, of the time of Ptolemy V, and from Mantinea.[24] The Roberts also assume that the grill was made of metal.[25]

In lines 10-11, we have the strange expression: κῆπος σὺν τῷ πεπηγμένῳ ξυλικῷ. The garden is perfectly to be expected in a temple enclosure, but the rest of the expression is obscure. The Roberts think of some kind of "travail en bois."[26] The rest becomes more

the need for much scholarly head-scratching. For example, Robert ignores Modern Greek usage when he refers to τὰ ἀδέλφια as a "mot de parenté très rare," *Opera Minora Selecta*, I, 423. This term and other neuter plurals that embrace both male and female relatives are extremely common in Modern Greek.

[23] Mr. Francis Piejko of Utica, N.Y., has been so kind as to furnish me by letter various suggestions that he has for the restoration of this inscription. For the first part of line 7 he proposes [στρωμνὴν τὴ]ν μέσην. This carries out the idea of details of furniture. The word is used *SIG*, 589.44 (= *Inschriften von Magnesia*, 98) of a lectisternium: στρωνύτω δὲ καὶ στρωμνὰς τρεῖς ὡς καλλίστας. (Interestingly enough, this occurs only one line before the ἀκροάματα which inspired the restoration in the Sounion inscription, discussed above.) If we can assume that in our no. 121 there were also three gods worshipped, as in the Magnesia inscription (Zeus Sosipolis, Artemis Leucophryene, and Apollo Pythius), then some sense may be made of the adjective μέση. Men may have been here part of a triad of gods, the central or principal one. It must be admitted, however, that no certain instance is known of Men's being part of a triad, and all this remains nothing more than speculative suggestion. Μέση may simply refer to the position of the στρωμνή or whatever inside the *peribolos*.

[24] Egypt: *OGIS*, 92; Mantinea: *IG*, V, ii, 268.

[25] *Op. cit.*, p. 49.

[26] But it seems to me that Mr. Piejko is on a more logical track, even if parallels for the precise word-usage escape him, in translating "a garden with planted trees."

obscure. In lines 11-12, θησαυρ[ὸν......]ον seems to appear, as befits a temple which is so money-conscious. An adjective describing the material is possible: [λίθιν]ον or [χάλκε]ον are both suggested by Robert. Bean suggests θησαυρ[οφυλάκι]ον.[27]

In lines 12-13, we have what Bean restores as ξυλοθ[ήκ]η costing six denarii. A wood-box, therefore, for the sacrificial fires. Bean's reading, not contested by the Roberts, seems guaranteed by the traces of the letters.[28]

Finally, in lines 13-14, we have a crux. Robert read: τοὺς βωμοὺς [...ὁμ]οῦ ὑφ' ἕν. Bean is right in pointing out that ὁμοῦ ὑφ' ἕν is highly redundant, but his own suggestion, even based as it is on a better reading of the preserved letter-traces: βωμοὺς [τ]οῦ ε[ἰργ]μοῦ seems hardly any better, as εἰργμός would be totally unparalleled as meaning anything but "prison." The Roberts therefore are correct in being doubtful, and I think the question must remain open.[29]

All in all, then, in spite of all the uncertainties, we seem to have a temple in which banquets regularly took place, which had a garden, easy chairs, and altars, as well as a place to store wood for the sacrifices, and which, unlike any Men-shrine that we know of except that mentioned in no. 155 (for the restoration νόμισμα οὑγκιαῖον in the Sounion inscription is hardly to be accepted), regularly collected and stored money.

Turning now to the priesthoods mentioned in the preserved material — it would seem that a priesthood would presuppose a place of worship also — let us examine first those in which the reference is fairly simple.

We have already mentioned two of these instances, no. A6 (Comana Cappadociae) in which a ἱερεύς and a νεωκόρος presumably of Men are mentioned, and no. 121 (near Burdur), mentioning a πάρεδρος of Men. No. 129, from near ancient Andeda, mentions a

[27] Again, Mr. Piejko, thinking not so much of a concrete strongbox as of an endowment (cf. mon. no. 178), suggests θησαυρ[ὸν ἱκαν]όν.

[28] Mr. Piejko, following his general idea of an endowment, wants to read: εἰς ξύλων ὠνήν, but I do not think the traces of the letters can possibly be made to support this interpretation.

[29] On the next to last line, Mr. Piejko wants to restore: [ἄψαι ἀργυρί]ου. This is grammatically very awkward, where you would expect the article governing the infinitive to precede τοὺς βωμούς, but may just be correct, if Bean's readings of the letter-traces may be rejected.

certain Quintus Numerius (perhaps another freedman of a local Roman landowner, at least a Roman citizen)[30] who describes himself as a ἱερεὺς Μηνὸς Οὐρανίου. In accordance with an oracle (κατὰ χρηματισμόν) he is here dedicating at altar to θεὸς ὕψιστος.[31]

In no. 131, which consists of two curved blocks from the inner entablature of a circular or exedra-like building, there is an honorific inscription, presumably set up by the people of Anaboura, honoring an unnamed person, son of Touliandos, and hereditary priest of Men Askaenos. This man was wealthy and important enough to be described as [φι]λόπατρις κα[ὶ εὐεργέτης]. He seems therefore to have been a local dignitary of some importance, and even more than the πάρεδρος of no. 121 he was able to make benefactions to his community.

Another priest, presumably of Men, who was in a position to make public benefactions, was the giver of the theater-seat, no. 103, Apollonius, son of Menis III, Mesanbrius, at Ormeleis. Although he describes himself merely as ἱερατεύων, he dedicates the seat as a vow to Men Τολησέων. This is, incidentally, remarkable as a dedication of a vow, not in a temple, but of a usable object in a more secular context.[32]

From Aphrodisias, we know something about the activities of Callicrates, son of Molossos, priest of Men Askaenos and Hermes Agoraios. At some time not too late in the imperial period, judging by the letter forms, he went around restoring old monuments dedicated by his family, as well as dedicating new ones. Two assumptions are valid — first that these priesthoods were held by a citizen of some wealth and importance in the community, and that

---

[30] See, Levick, *RE*, Suppl. 12, s.v. *Andeda*, cols. 79 and 81. The name is there erroneously given as Numerianus.

[31] Both of these points are of interest, and I will return to them later. For the word χρηματισμός see Robert, *Hellenica*, 2, 1946, p. 72, note 1 and p. 148; *REG*, 74, 1961, p. 244, no. 748.

[32] But is the object dedicated necessarily a *theater*-seat, as has been generally assumed? Furniture occupies a large place among dedications to Men, and if you can trust Ramsay (no. AD7) there exists an instance of another seat being dedicated to Men in an out-building of a temple at Antioch in Pisidia.

The word Mesanbrios seems to be an ethnic, but Collignon's connection of it in the original publication with Mesembria in Thrace seems far-fetched.

the family had been of importance for some generations. Although no mention is made of a hereditary priesthood of Men or Hermes, it is significant that the forefather honored in the restored inscription no. 118[33] is recorded to have been a priest of Hecate, a divinity sometimes associated with Men.

In no. 120, we again have Callicrates restoring one of his forebears' monuments, a statue of Nike and a lion dedicated to the deified emperors and the people, whereas in no. 119, he apparently makes his own dedication, this time to Heracles and the people, of a table.[34] Although I doubt if any particularly close relationship can be assumed to have existed between the cult of Heracles and that of Men, at least in this highly officialized context no discrepancy was seen in a priest of Men making a dedication to Heracles.

Finally, to round out this picture of official priesthoods in the cities of Asia Minor, we have no. 101, an honorary degree of the people of Eumeneia for one [Μ. Αὐρ.] Μόνιμος Ἀρίστων[ος Ζηνόδοτ]ος. If the restoration Αὐρ. is correct, the inscription is from after the time of the Constitutio Antoniniana. The right-hand side of the inscription is lost, but it is still certain that Monimos held many priesthoods at Eumeneia, as well as civic offices, such as *agoranomos* and others conjecturally restored. The divinities with whom Men seems to be associated in Monimos' career are Zeus Soter, Apollo, Mother Agdistis, Agathos Daimon, and Sebaste Eirene. The honorand is also described as *lampadarches*, apparently a function concerned with religious festivals, as it is mentioned in the first part of the inscription, that concerned with his priesthoods.[35]

We are, however, in quite a different realm with this inscription and with no. 131, if correctly restored, than we were with the Lydian inscriptions. There, for all the abundance of the material, and all it

---

[33] A pre-imperial original of this inscription seems to exist, *BCH*, 9, 1885, p. 74, no. 5.

[34] See the discussion of tables above, in connection with the Sounion inscriptions.

[35] We must ask ourselves also in no. A9, whether the priest Menelaos, whose son, daughter-in-law, and grandson dedicate a statue (?) of Men Patalaos to the *demos* of Serivada, was a priest of Men. If so, he can join the roster of well-to-do ones.

In connection with the term *lampadarches*, see what I have to say below about the association of Men and Demeter.

told us about the inner psychology of the cult, we found only one priestess, and she was honored, not publicly, but by the καταλουστικοί, not for civic services, but for her unselfish devotion to the god and goodness towards men. How different are the inscriptions of Anaboura, Aphrodisias (where Men is also known, though sparingly, from the numismatic sources), and Eumeneia! Here the priesthood of Men is connected with being a member of a prominent, wealthy, and civic-minded family, and there is correspondingly a lack of emphasis on the psychological aspects of the cult.

Together with the official temples and priesthoods, would seem to go asyla. The whole city of Sillyon, which is one of the best represented of all cities among the numismatic evidence for Men, proudly proclaims itself on its last coinage, in the reign of the emperor Aurelian, to be Θεοῦ Μηνὸς ἄσυλον, and we know also from monument no. 130, from Apollonia Pisidiae (known also as an issuer of Men-coins, although sparingly) of one specific asylum of Men, presumably a temple precinct.[36]

Before we leave the general topic of the cult in Asia Minor excluding Lydia and Pisidian Antioch, two further local phenomena need to be discussed. One is the role of Men, particularly Μὴν Καταχθόνιος, in the protection of graves, and the other is the phenomenon of facelessness.

Men as protector of graves is known from two areas: Lydia, and Lycaonia-Cilicia. Two of the Lydian inscriptions (nos. 70 and 71) we have already had occasion to refer to, in regard to the use of the word ἁμαρτάνω, and in the latter case also in regard to the preventive function of placing a scepter on an altar. In other respects also these two inscriptions follow the model of the majority of Maeonian Men-inscriptions, in the use of the epithet *Axiottenos*, and in the association of Men with Anaeitis (no. 71 only).

No. 70, however, has the formula, τεύξηται τοῦ Ἀξιοττηνοῦ κεχολωμένου which it shares, not only with the Lycaonian inscriptions, but

[36] L. Robert, *Hellenica*, 6, 1948, p. 34 ff., discusses at length asylum-precincts in various cults. I am not convinced by the suggestion of A. H. M. Jones, cited by Barbara Levick, *Roman Colonies in Southern Asia Minor*, Oxford, 1967, p. 216, note 4, that the asylum-stone of Apollonia may have had some connection with the great temple of Antioch. There were too many small local sanctuaries of Men for one to need recourse to such a hypothesis.

also with no. 81, from Sardis, which reads, in L. Robert's restoration:

[......Μ]ηνὸς Τυμωλεί[του]
[καὶ τῶν θεῶν τ]ῶν ἄλλων πάν[των]
[κεχολωμένων] τύχοιτο.[37]

The remaining funerary inscriptions are all of the general Lycaonian area: nos. 143-151; 154-156; A5; and perhaps AD5 and AD6, although the relationship of the last-named to any recognizable form of the Men-cult is very puzzling. Perhaps to these can be added no. 153, identified as a grave monument by the snake shown on its side, although at first glance this monument is simply a votive altar to θεὸς Οὐινδιεινός, whom the relief shows to be identical with Men.[38]

The run of these inscriptions is the following: After a statement of who is buried there, Men is adjured[39] to protect the tomb, both against damage,[40] and against anyone being buried in it without permission,[41] or against anyone buying or selling the tomb.[42] The punishment is to have Men angry.[43] In two instances, a pecuniary

[37] See my article in *Numen* for possible propaganda value which the Romans may have extracted from an epithet such as *Tymoleites*. For general connections of the moon with the sojourn of the dead, see Cumont's chapter, "La Lune Séjour des Morts," in his *Recherches sur le Symbolisme Funéraire des Romains*, Paris, 1942. The function of protecting graves, however, was not exclusively entrusted to lunar divinities, and we have very similar wording to our inscriptions in those from the area of Cibyra which invoke the Θεοὶ Πισιδικοί, see Roscher's *Lexikon*, s.v.; L. Robert, *Villes d'Asie Mineure*, Paris, 1935, p. 213.

[38] For the snake as an indication that we are dealing with a grave-monument, see Wide, *ARW*, 12, 1909, p. 221 ff. An altar is indicated to be a part of the grave furniture on a number of sepulchral inscriptions involving Men in this area — nos. 145, 150, and 155. This seems to have been the role played by no. 153, although in combining the votive and funerary functions it resembles the odd inscription published by Ramsay, *Bearing*, pp. 188-190. On the words λάρναξ and βωμός in the epigraphy of the area, see Robert, *Hellenica*, 13, 1964, 240 ff. See also Kubinska, *Les Monuments Funéraires dans les Inscriptions Grecques d'Asie Mineure*, Warsaw, 1968, index, where a distinction is drawn between two meanings of βωμός, "altar" or "platform."

[39] Ἐνορκῶ or the like — nos. 143, 144, 148, 155, A5, AD5.
[40] Nos. 144-147, 149, A5, AD6.
[41] Nos. 143-145, 147, 148, 150, 155, AD5.
[42] No. 156.
[43] Nos. 145-147, 149-151, 154, AD5, AD6.

penalty is attached to the divine wrath: In no. 144, the wrongdoer is to give 5000 denarii to the temple (presumably a money-collecting temple like that of no. 121). And in no. 147, according to Cronin's restoration, he is to give 2500 denarii to the fiscus (at least the 500 part of the figure is certain).[44]

Most interesting, however, in this context, are the changes in Men's epithets, in the gods that accompany him, and, most remarkably of all, in his number.

The commonest appellation for Men, as one might expect, is simply Καταχθόνιος (nos. 143, 145, 146, 148-150). In one example (no. 151) this is shortened to mere Χθόνιος. In one other (no. 147, heavily restored) Μὴν Κατακθόνιος appears to be associated with some unspecified θεοὶ καταχθόνιοι. The other inscriptions are more surprising. In no. A5, Men is both Καταχθόνιος and Οὐράνιος, thus adding an epithet which occurs sporadically for Men as far west as Attica, and the meaning of which is obvious.[45] There does not seem to be any question, yet, but that Men is singular. The situation is changed, however, in no. 144, which speaks of Μῆνας Καταχθονίους; in no. 156, which speaks of Μῆνας Οὐράνιον καὶ Καταχθονίους; and no. 155, which speaks of τρῖς θ[εοὺς] Μῆνας, apparently the same, one heavenly and two of the underworld, as those referred to in no. 156.[46] A further example of the same idea is furnished in no. 154, Μῆνα ἄνωθεν καὶ κάτο[θεν].[47]

---

[44] In no. 144, the ε' is to be taken as 5000, instead of five, unless it can be assumed that a terrific inflation took place between the times of the two inscriptions. (No. 121 would seem to be preinflationary, if τ' is taken as meaning 300, rather than 300,000.) The editors use the word *drachmai* for the monetary unit, but this is an equivalent expression for *denarii*. For both these points, see L. Robert, *Hellenica*, 13, p. 211. *Fiscus* would point to the imperial treasury, rather than a temple, and is adequately attested with parallels. Cf. Bean and Mitford, *Journeys in Rough Cilicia*, Österreichische Akademie der Wissenschaften, Denkschriften, Phil.-Hist. Klasse, 102, no. 226; Robert, *Hellenica*, 13, p. 205. The imperial treasury can also be called τὸ ἱερώτατον ταμεῖον, Robert, *Opera Minora Selecta*, III, p. 428.

[45] Compare the Ἥλιος Πλούτων of no. 28.

[46] The only monument outside this area which seems to acknowledge plural Mens, in its text, if not in its relief, is the Lydian inscription no. 53.

[47] Cf. Καταχθονία Σελήνη in Bean and Mitford, *op. cit.*, no. 266 from Mut-Claudiopolis, and Σελήνη φαίνουσα in the same role, *ibid.*, no. 240. As so often the sex of the moon-divinity is unimportant. This point will be discussed further below.

W. M. Calder, however, republished our no. 155[48] and read

ἐνορκῶ τρὶς θ'
Μῆνας ἀνεπιλύτους.

He backed up this interpretation, not only with the fact that he could find no space after the theta on the stone, but with two other inscriptions, which we have published as AD5 and AD6. I do not find his concept of 9 or even 27 Mens as particularly likely although in this cult little would surprise me.[49] I would suggest that AD6, where the reading is highly uncertain anyhow, be left out of the discussion until such time as it can be checked out. In AD5, there can be no doubt as to the ἐννέα, even though [τ]ρίς is less certain from the photo. But we can accept both this and Calder's reading of no. 155 with a lot less trouble if we do not view τρὶς ἐννέα as a cardinal numeral telling us the number of Mens, but rather as meaning τρὶς ἐνάκις, and giving the magic number of times that a more limited, if unspecified, number of Mens, were called upon to protect the grave. At all events, it remains a local peculiarity of Savatra, and should not be extrapolated to monuments from elsewhere.

To turn to the other local peculiarity mentioned above, the motif of facelessness is encountered on nos. 104, 121, 124, 127 and 128, as well as possibly on others, such as nos. 87, 107, and 125. Those that definitely represent this phenomenon are from a limited area to the south of the Lake of Burdur, and thus represent a distinct local variation in iconography. The observation that the facelessness of these representations was deliberate, and not the result of wear, was first made by G. E. Bean.[50] To my knowledge, no commentator has ventured to elucidate the matter. The only explanation that comes to my mind is that the god is considered as being too brilliant to behold. The very brilliance of his face prohibits our distinguishing his features, and thus in a naive way these reliefs attempt to convey that fact. The parallelism with Judeo-Christian conceptions is again too obvious to need pointing out.

---

[48] *MAMA*, VII, no. 234a.
[49] L. Robert mentions these inscriptions in *Hellenica*, 13, *passim*, but remains strangely silent on this striking theological point.
[50] *Anatolian Studies*, 9, 1959, p. 73, in regard to our no. 124.

CHAPTER FOUR

THE CULT AT ANTIOCH IN PISIDIA

Antioch in Pisidia ranks unquestionably as the greatest center of Men-cult in antiquity. The cult there reaches back before Roman times, although it is impossible to say just how far. Strabo can write of Antioch:[1]

῏Ην δὲ ἐνταῦθα καὶ ἱεροσύνη τις Μηνὸς ᾿Ασκαίου, πλῆθος ἔχουσα ἱεροδούλων καὶ χωρίων ἱερῶν. Κατελύθη δὲ μετὰ τὴν ᾿Αμύντου τελευτὴν ὑπὸ τῶν πεμφθέντων ἐπὶ τὴν ἐκείνου κληρονομίαν.

The early importance of Men-cult in Antioch is also attested by the pre-Roman coinage.[2] These coins bear a bust of Men on the obverse, and on the reverse, either a humped bull and magistrate's name, or a figure of Nike with a palm-branch, also with the magistrate's name. It is impossible to venture any dating of these coins in the present state of our evidence, except that they can be placed between the freeing of Antioch from Seleucid rule, by the treaty of Apamea (188 B.C.), and the transformation of the Galatian kingdom into a Roman province by Augustus in 25 B.C. These coins do, however, indicate to us that even at this early period Men was associated not only with the bull, but with the idea of victory, with which he appears regularly in the typical Antiochene representation, apparently derived from his cult-image, from the time of Antoninus Pius onwards. It may well be an Antiochene from this Antioch who is mentioned in the probably Hellenistic inscription from Rhodes, no. 17.

The original Seleucid settlers were from Magnesia on the Maeander,[3] and Men is worshipped in that city also,[4] so it may be that the cults in the two cities are connected. But since the earliest Men-

---

[1] XII, viii, 14 (= T. 2).
[2] *CMRDM*, II, Antioch nos. 1-17.
[3] Strabo, *loc. cit.* (= T. 2).
[4] *CMRDM*, I, no. 29; nine coin-types in *CMRDM*, II.

coins of Magnesia are of the Severan period, and since both places have a very peculiar and pronounced iconography, the one quite different from the other, it is probably best to postulate independent development in the two places.

Strabo uses a very strong word (κατελύθη) to describe the fate of the cult of Men at the time of the Roman colonization by Augustus. The temple had come to possess extensive land-holdings and slave-holdings by the time Augustus made Galatia a province, and this all seems to have been broken up, the land, it can reasonably be supposed, going to provide farms for the Roman colonists.[5]

I have suggested elsewhere[6] that perhaps the Romans chose their new colony, not only in order to hold their new province militarily, but also for the propaganda value which could be drawn from its principal cult. This is speculative. Certainly, the secular possessions of the temple were broken up, and the Romans may have been slow to realize the potential that Men-cult had for propaganda value. We cannot tell. The earliest definite sign of Roman exploitation of Men-cult for propaganda is the Galba-coin which we have listed as, "Uncertain, perhaps Ancyra."[7] The earliest full recrudescence of Men-cult in Antioch, its beginning to regain its former status, is signalled by the coinage of the reign of Antoninus Pius.[8] There does exist a series of smaller coins, some portraying Men, which are undatable (*CMRDM*, II, Antioch 18-23) and which may bridge this period, as well as inscription no. 160, which is apparently of first-century date. Significantly, however, Krzyzanowska[9] wishes to date the earliest of these small coins contemporaneously with Antoninus Pius also.

The type of Men shown on the coins with imperial obverses, with the attributes of Nike, bucranium, and rooster, continues in use through the reign of Volusian, and is clearly derived from the local cult-statue. This cult-statue also gave rise to a miniature copy of itself, found in the sanctuary on the top of Kara Kuyu (monument no. 175). One coin-type of Gordian III (Antioch no. 56) shows the

[5] See Barbara Levick, *Roman Colonies in Southern Asia Minor*, p. 72 ff.
[6] *Numen*, 22, 1975, p. 236.
[7] *CMRDM*, II, p. 160.
[8] *CMRDM*, II, Antioch 24.
[9] *Monnaies Coloniales d'Antioche de Pisidie*, Warsaw, 1970, Pl. V, Table 8.

statue inside its temple. The fact that this type, localized in one temple at Antioch, was copied in other cities, even as distant as Ancyra, shows the importance which Antioch had as a center for diffusion of the cult.[10]

The Romans seem to have been perplexed as to how to render the name of this male moon-god into their language. On the coins of Antoninus Pius (nos. 25, 26), the word Μήν is rendered into Latin with its normal meaning of "month," and comes out *Mensis*. This continues sporadically on some dies until the time of Septimius Severus and his family (nos. 37, 38, 44, 51), but on one of them (no. 39) the engraver gives up all pretense of writing Latin and treats the coin inscription as if it were a Greek vow, by writing Μηνί. More remarkable is the coin of Caracalla (no. 48), on which Men is accompanied by the inscription *Fortuna Col. Antioch*. This may be a simple engraver's blunder, as the figure of Fortuna (Tyche) appears in the same series of coins.[11] On the other hand, it may be influenced by the fact that Men was indeed the tutelary divinity of the city. One is reminded of the close relationship between Men and Tyche on the coins of Nysa, and on the alliance coins of Temenothyrae with Sebaste and with Bagis.

Later, however, the Romans seem to have preferred to overlook awkwardness of gender than awkwardness of meaning, and render Men as *Luna*. The best example of this is the honorary inscription (monument no. 178) for Caius Albucius Firmus, who gave money for the gymnastic contests to be held *diebus festis Lunae*. More often, however, the difficulty of gender is abbreviated out of the way by the formula *LVS*, which closely corresponds to Μηνὶ εὐχήν on the votive inscriptions.[12] It seems clear that these letters are to be taken

[10] Specifically the Antiochene type appears on Julia 3, Lysinia 1, parlais 1, Siblia 4-5, Ancyra 7, 10, 13, and 15, and, apart from coins, on gem G6.

[11] Krzyzanowska, *op. cit.*, Plate XI.

[12] *LVS* occurs on nos. 160, 176, 200, 205, 213, 222, 227, 231, 236, 249, 250, 256, 257, 261. I first proposed the present interpretation of it, *Berytus*, 15, 1964, p. 30. It has now been accepted, if hesitantly, by Barbara Levick, *AS*, 20, 1970, pp. 49-50. The traditional interpretation as *Libens Votum Solvit* falls down for several reasons:

1. The more usual V(otum) S(olvit) L(ibens) M(erito) does not occur at Antioch.
2. The correspondence between *LVS* and Μηνὶ εὐχήν.

as meaning "Lunae Votum Solvit." The abbreviation has the great advantage of obscuring the awkwardness of the gender.

A temple of Men was located on a hill outside the city, called Kara Kuyu.[13] This has the distinction of being the only temple of Men so far brought to light. Unfortunately, the main publication of it is by W. M. Ramsay,[14] who had partly excavated it in the summer of 1912. As is so often the case, Ramsay's presentation of the evidence is so inextricably tied up with questionable, preconceived, and far-fetched interpretations, that it is hard to know just what was really there and what he imagined. More reliable information is given by Margaret Hardie (Hasluck),[15] but her article, our main source for the inscriptions of the peribolos-wall, is by no means a full excavation-report, although it does give a general description of the site, with dimensions.[16]

I visited the site myself in 1961, and my conclusions and observations have been published.[17] I am unable to add anything new to the discussion now. The site is crying out for an adequate and responsible archaeological reexamination. Until that is done and an

3. No. 250 has *LVSLM*, which if resolved L(ibens) V(otum) S(olvit) L(ibens) M(erito) would be redundant. The first L must therefore have another meaning. No. 227 is also redundant on the traditional interpretation.

4. Influence of the abbreviation-loving Latin epigraphy on the Greek is seen particularly in no. 268, where *MAE* corresponds to *LVS*. It is to be resolved: Μηνὶ Ἀσκαηνῷ εὐχήν.

The form *Lunus*, frequently used for Men in modern sources, is attested in antiquity only in *Scriptores Historiae Augustae*, Caracalla, VII, à propos of that emperor's fatal visit to temple of Sin at Carrhae. It is impossible to tell whether the author of that life had any real knowledge that this compromise form was actually in use for Men during the period of his worship at Antioch.

[13] A notice in Strabo, XII, viii, 14 = T. 2 seems to indicate that there were two temples of Men, one near Antioch, and one in its territory. But this does not jibe with information given by Strabo, XII, iii, 31 = T. 1, and Barbara Levick has suggested (*JHS*, 91, 1971, p. 81) that the temple in the territory may be a ghost caused by a corruption of the text. Over the course of the years, this ghost, if it is one, has given scholars a lot of trouble and exercise in trying to find it. The Ramsay-Anderson hypothesis sees it as being at Sağir, where the Tekmoreian inscriptions were found, in spite of the absence of Men from that location.

[14] *ABSA*, 18, 1911-12, pp. 37 ff.
[15] *JHS*, 32, 1912, p. 111 ff.
[16] See also Ramsay *JRS*, 4, 1918, p. 110 ff.
[17] *Berytus*, 15, 1964, p. 39 ff. with Plate VII.

architectural study made of the remains, any further discussion is premature.

The site has, however, yielded considerable epigraphical evidence, which is itself informative. It falls into two major categories, the inscriptions cut into the peribolos-wall (nos. 179-244, 248, 252), and those cut onto stones of better quality, more durable, which could be set up in the sanctuary (nos. 176-177, 245-247, 249-251, 253-294, A4, A10). A special place seems to be occupied by no. 160, far and away the earliest of the lot — the others, insofar as they can be dated, seem to be of the later third century —, a dedication by a freedman of Claudius, who now held an important point at Antioch, set up at the request of his parents. The first category, being roughly cut into very poor quality stone, are hard to read (at the time of my visit in 1961 they were covered with mud, weeds, etc.) and suffer from the amoeba-like quality of so much that Ramsay worked with. A prime example of the differences in reading that can occur is given by no. 193; or by the fact that 190 and 195b are actually the same;[18] or that 242 was later reread by Ramsay as follows:

Κυρίῳ Μηνὶ εὐχήν,
Μακεδὼν κτλ.[19]

The free-standing stones, however, are more reliable. Many of them eventually found their way into the museums at Constantinople (176-177), Yalvaç (253-255), Aberdeen (259), or Konya (162, 249-250, 260-294, A4), where it has been possible to study them to greater advantage. None of this material is dated; however, the letter-forms and general context point to a date in the second half of the third century A.D.

What conclusions emerge from a consideration of these monuments? For one thing, making dedications to Men could be repeated — no. 253 (fourth time), no. 264 (second time). It was very often a family affair, resembling Men's role as protector of the family in

[18] See *CMRDM*, II, p. 172.
[19] Ruge in *RE*, s.v. *Tekmoreioi Xenoi*, col. 169, citing a letter from Ramsay. Μακεδών is entirely possible — presumably descended from one of the original Seleucid settlers. Cf. nos. 276 and 285. For Μὴν κύριος, cf. nos. 43 and A6.

the Attic material. Family members mentioned are brothers, sisters, children, wives, cousins, and foster-children, who are unusually common in these inscriptions.[20]

Another very striking feature is the use of the word τεκμορεύσας.[21] An analysis of this list shows that there is considerable overlap between the inscriptions involving families and those using the word τεκμορεύσας. Like simple vows, the action implied by τεκμορεύσας could be repeated: no. 262 (third time).[22] Or a woman could be τεκμορεύσασα by herself, without family-members (289), just as she could be the prime or sole dedicant of a simple vow (189, perhaps 193).[23]

Unfortunately, we do not know what the word τεκμορεύσας means. It would seem certainly to have some kind of connection with the Xenoi Tekmoreioi, lists of whose members and their contributions are known from Sağir and Kumdanlı, villages to the north of Antioch.[24] They are a group of people, whose activities are datable from ca. 238 to ca. 265 A.D., resident in various parts of Asia Minor, who make contributions, set up dedications on behalf of the emperor, worship Artemis, and apparently enjoy a communal meal, as their most characteristic official is named πρωτανακλιτής. Ruge, following Ramsay, certainly seems to be right in suggesting[25] that one of the members is specifically noted as τεκμορεύσας δίς, because all of them were already τεκμορεύσαντες once. The mere fact, however, that this action was held to be commendable, both in the cult of Men and in that of Artemis still does not tell us what it consisted

---

[20] The following are all dedications by more than one family member: 177, 180, 181, 184, 189, 191, 194, 199, 202-204, 218, 210, 211, 219, 226-230, 233, 239, 241-245, 247, 252-254, 256-261, 263, 264, 268 (unique in the use of ὑπέρ), 270, 273, 274, 277, 279-281, 283, 287, 288, 291, 293, A4. For θρεπτοί see Cameron, in *Anatolian Studies Presented to W. H. Buckler*, Manchester, 1939, pp. 27-62, and Nani, *Epigraphica*, 5-6, 1943-44, pp. 45-48.

[21] It occurs in nos. 177, 180, 191, 192, 203, 208, 212, 228, 240-242, 244-247, 252-254, 259, 260, 262-266, 271-275, 279-281, 283, 284, 287, 289-294, A4.

[22] Cf. also Ruge, *art. cit.*, no. 4, line 34.

[23] The only other similar cult-use of an aorist participle that comes to mind is the use of ναυαρχήσας in some Isis-Sarapis inscriptions. Cf. particularly Vidman, *SIRIS*, no. 82, from Eretria.

[24] See particularly Ruge, *RE*, 2nd series V, 1934, col. 158 ff., *s.v. Tekmoreioi Xenoi*; Levick, *JHS*, 91, 1971, p. 83.

[25] *Art. cit.*, col. 167.

of. Ramsay,[26] in an extremely frustrating article in which he refers to inscriptions by number without ever publishing the texts, claims to have in one of them the paraphrase τέκμορ ποίσας, but this does not help us much. The word must have the basic idea of "sign," but what the sign is, or what was done with it, remains unknown. Ramsay fantasized that the action of τεκμορεύειν consisted of holding up a crescent-shaped object to an image of the god,[27] but Ruge is right in pointing out the baselessness of these speculations.[28] For one thing, no crescents are present on the inscriptions of the Xenoi Tekmoreioi, and for another, crescents are all over the Men-dedications of Antioch, whether they use the word τεκμορεύσας or not. Therefore the idea of τεκμορεύειν must be dissociated from the idea of the crescent, and we must simply admit that we do not know what it was. It could be, however, that in the cult at Antioch as well as among the *Xenoi*, the action involved a money-payment, and this accounts for the colony's appointing *curatores arcae sanctuarii*.[29]

If the crescent is not the τέκμωρ, it certainly is the omnipresent sign of Men on these inscriptions. An interesting fact is that the number of crescents often corresponds to the number of dedicants.[30] The shape of the crescents is also worth our attention. In a number of cases they appear with lugs at the bottom, as if for insertion into a holder.[31] The suggestion has been advanced[32] that this lugged crescent represents a degenerate bull's head, but as I have observed elsewhere,[33] this supposition does not seem to have any real merit.

[26] *JRS*, 8, 1918, p. 138.
[27] *Art. cit.*, p. 141.
[28] *Art. cit.*, col. 168.
[29] See Levick, *Roman Colonies*, p. 85.
[30] Already observed by Levick, *Anatolian Studies*, 20, 1970, p. 39. In the following instances, the number of crescents corresponds to the number of dedicants: nos. 177, 179, 180, 184, 188, 189, 192, 194-200, 202-204, 207, 208, 210, 214, 224, 227, 229-231, 236-239, 243, 245, 248, 253, 264, 266, 270, 281, 287, 288, 290. There are admittedly some unquestionable counterexamples, such as nos. 241, 242, 244, and 291, in which the number of dedicants and the number of crescents cannot possibly be squared.
[31] Examples are provided by nos. 182, 183, 187, 192, 195, 197, 199, 201-203, 206, 209, 214, 215, 217-219, 221, 224-226, 229, 230, 232, 239, 241, 264.
[32] Hardie, *art. cit.*, p. 117.
[33] *Berytus*, 15, 1964, p. 38, note 138.

It is to be noted that many of the rock-cut inscriptions are themselves little imitation steles, complete with lugs at the bottom for insertion into a base (*e.g.*, nos. 195a, 209, 221). A similar origin can also probably be suggested for the appendages that appear together with the bottom lug on nos. 96 (Nacoleia), 269, and 285, as well as without the bottom lug on no. 115 (Julia). This phenomenon, which also occurs on a Sabazius-Men syncretistic statuette which I have published[34] occurs also on monuments of the western provinces, and has been commented on by F. Cumont,[35] who concludes that both the bottom lug and the appendages arise from practical considerations (the appendages from a desire to prevent injury or breakage) in the case of free-standing crescents, which are then imitated on the reliefs. (Admittedly, none of the supposed free-standing crescents seem to have been preserved.)

If then these crescents have already so lost contact with realistic representations of actual crescent moons, and if details originally intended to be practical have become decorative, it should come as no surprise that other decorative elements add themselves to crescents in various places: no. 261 (central line dividing the crescent lengthwise); no. 93 (central line and ivy leaves); no. 115 (blob in the middle).[36]

To return to the Antiochene epigraphy: Another characteristic of the free-standing reliefs is the use of a wreath. Elsewhere it occurs only on the two Lydian funerary inscriptions, nos. 70 and 71, where, of course, the wreath is at home. In the Antiochene votive inscriptions it occurs twelve times.[37] The wreath, usually tied with a ribbon and surrounding a crescent (once the effigy of Men, no. 282) would seem here not to have funereal significance, but to be connected with the age old motif of victory, particularly the victory holding a

---

[34] *Muse*, 8, 1974, pp. 34-37.

[35] *Recherches*, p. 222.

[36] For ivy leaves, cf. the Spanish monuments, Cumont, *op. cit.*, figs. 57 and 60.

[37] Nos. 249, 250, 253, 261, 266, 267, 271, 282, 283, 287, 291, and 293. Cf. also the wreath-like object around the bucranium of no. 110, from Vetissus. One wonders whether there may be any connection with the hitherto unexplained looped band of coin no. 53.

wreath, present on coins of Antioch from pre-Imperial times and joined closely with Men in the Antiochene cult-statue.

The wreath is certainly more than a purely decorative motif. Who is victorious? The god or the worshipper? And over what? The forces of evil, sin, or even death? Much eludes us in the present state of our evidence, but I will try to elucidate this matter as far as I am able in the chapter on iconography.

Closely connected with the idea of victory, of course, is the idea of actual contests. Here we are well informed at Antioch. These games are attested in inscriptions nos. 161, and 164-174.[38] It is my feeling, also, that inscription no. 178 is to be related to this group of inscriptions. At some fairly early time in the history of the colony, when Latin was still in extensive use[39] Caius Albucius Firmus left money by his will for a *certamen gymnicum* to be held annually *diebus festis Lunae*.[40] Perhaps the early lists of victors[41] can be assigned to this earlier festival.

Later in the imperial period, the games seem to have been revived. The fragmentary inscription published by Anderson,[42] written in Greek with late letter forms, a few words of Latin thrown in (all that remained as a vestige of the colonial city government of Antioch, now thoroughly Hellenized), seems to be an official decree of the city, honoring G. Ulpius Baebianus for making a gift to the city. Since the same man appears as the presiding priest in the agonistic inscriptions nos. 164-167, the assumption is that he also made the gift[43] that allowed the games to be reinstituted with greater splendor.

---

[38] In addition, Anderson, *JRS*, 1913, p. 281 ff. publishes a number of lists of victors, apparently earlier than the bulk of the material, which I excluded from *CMRDM*, I, because no explicit mention of Men is made in them. Anderson, *op. cit.*, fig. 48, inscription 3, *may*, however, have some bearing on Men-cult, but it cannot be told whether the letters μην- that appear are part of the god's name, a personal name, or a dating formula.

[39] Cf. the Roman difficulty with the name of Men, discussed above. The sex of the moon-divinity is relatively unimportant. This is why Strabo can call Men, Selene (XII, iii, 31 = T. 1); this is the proper explanation, not that given by Anderson, p. 272.

[40] Anderson, *op. cit.*, p. 281 ff., nos. 7-10a.

[41] *Op. cit.*, p. 284 ff., figs. 60-61.

[42] His name appears, frag. a, line 6.

[43] Frag. f, line 7; the gift was at least 20,000 Attic drachmas.

The use of the word *Caesares*,[44] together with the description of the contest as Μαξιμιάνειος,[45] leads Anderson to date the games to after the institution of the tetrarchy in A.D. 293. All this argumentation is somewhat tenuous, but not inherently improbable.[46]

Turning now to the agonistic inscriptions themselves: They refer to Men as *Patrios* (nos. 164-174), an epithet also occasionally encountered on the votive inscriptions (263, 290). This fits in well with the Roman propagandistic purpose of convincing people of the inherent Anatolianness of Men, as well as of his Roman connections — nor was the long history of the cult any exaggeration at Antioch in this period.

The games recorded on inscriptions 164-174 include not only gymnastic contests, but in one case (166) a contest of trumpeters. They were games with money prizes, as is indicated by the use of the word θέμις (the counting of θέμιδες is because "they were celebrated only a limited number of times, so long in fact as the individual donor continued to provide the money, or so long as the fund which he instituted by will lasted").[47] In one case the victor, a child wrestler, had also competed at Ancyra (no. 174). In another (no. 164) the victory was by default, after the other contestants saw the winner stripped for the contest. In two cases (nos. 170-171) an official called ἐπιστάτης is mentioned, although his exact functions are nowhere defined.[48]

---

[44] Frag. h, line 3.

[45] Nos. 166-168, 170-174.

[46] Anderson's article, however, is almost as frustratingly hard to use as are those of Ramsay. Not only is the presentation of evidence scrambled with the interpretation of evidence — perhaps in the present series of books I have gone to the other extreme in trying to keep them separate — but evidence is referred to in passing, without ever really being presented. For instance, I have never succeeded in finding out anything further about the alleged dedication to Men by Ulpius Baebianus and Ulpia Cornelia, mentioned by Anderson, p. 287.

[47] Anderson, *op. cit.*, p. 298. Cf. also L. Robert, *Etudes Anatoliennes*, p. 432 f. These inscriptions of course fit into a much larger theme of athletic contests throughout the Eastern Empire, about which much has been written and much is known. For our purposes, however, it must be regarded as a side-issue, and I do not intend to get involved in it here. Louis Robert has been particularly interested in agonistic inscriptions, and I refer the reader to his works.

[48] See also Anderson, p. 290, no. 19a.

As Anderson observes, the inscriptions fall into three categories. In the first, nos. 164-167, G. Ulpius Baebianus is sole agonothete. As well as giving money for this festival for life, he is also augur and lifetime priest of Men and Demeter (an association of gods to be discussed in detail below). Under his leadership, the games were celebrated at least seven times.[49] The next stage seems to be that under the double agonothetes for life, G. Caesennius Proclus Staianus and G. Flavius Baebianus (nos. 168-170). Of these two men, the former is described as augur and patron of the colony, the latter as a Roman knight and lifetime high priest of Men. In the last stage, characterized by the most carelessly incised inscriptions (171-174), G. Flavius Baebianus appears alone as agonothete for life, and is described as pontifex, patron of the colony, and lifetime high priest of Men. This stage went on for at least two years, as is shown by no. 174.[50]

The Maximian after whom the games were consistently named is convincingly identified by Anderson with Maximian Galerius. I do not, however, see the necessity for the assumption that the games were instituted only after Galerius' elevation to Augustus in 305. The favor and protection of a Caesar would, I think, be enough for the local games here. Furthermore, as the games were celebrated more years than those served by Galerius as Augustus, we would have to account for this more than usual faithfulness to the memory of a dead emperor.

In short, then, the cult at Antioch in Pisidia seems to be the quintessence of a public cult. Although the temple of Men lost its temporal importance when the Roman colony was sent out, the Romans do not seem to have been too long in becoming aware of the value of Men Askaenos as a god who could comfortably be worshipped both by the natives and by the colonists. By the time of Antoninus Pius, the cult seems to be back in full swing, and a cult-image of Men becomes one of the commonest badges of the colony on its coins. As well as the expected altar (163), a table (255) and perhaps a chair (AD7) are dedicated to Men, and perhaps

[49] No. 167 — θέμιδι ζ'.
[50] There is also a mysterious fragment, Anderson, p. 295, no. 25, which seems to speak of a sixteenth θέμις, if read correctly.

another table in the sanctuary,[51] giving us hints of aspects of the cult about which we are as yet uninformed. Nor do we know the purpose of a tub found in the sanctuary.[52] During the last stages of the cult, and perhaps earlier, games were held in Men's honor. The wreath of victory is from the earliest days associated with his worship at Antioch, although its exact meaning on the votive inscriptions remains unclear. The priests whom we know of, all from the latest stages of the cult, appear as rich grandees of the community, able to finance the games out of their own funds. Many dedications are set up, both in Greek and in Latin, but they are monotonous. They do show Men as protector of the family, and they show the importance of the action, whatever it may be, called τεκμορεύειν. Only the remarkable tablet no. 162, with its concentric squares of letters, shows any particular originality in trying to offer Men anything eye-catching or unusual.

[51] Lane, *Berytus*, 15, 1964, p. 41.
[52] Lane, *loc. cit.*

CHAPTER FIVE

THE EPITHETS OF MEN AND OTHER ADJECTIVES APPLIED TO HIM

One of the most striking characteristics of the Men-cult, as of other Anatolian cults, is the fact that his name so often is accompanied by an epithet or other adjective. The epithets fall into two categories: those in the form of a genitive (with or without a preposition), and those which adjectivally modify the name.[1]

That most of those in the genitive form are real genitives and give the name of the founder of a sanctuary, there can be little doubt. Such instances are:

Μὴν Ἀρτεμιδώρου (Ἀξιοττηνός) (nos. 33, 42, 47, 86 and A1);
Μὴν Ἀξιοττηνὸς ἐξ Ἀπολλωνίου (no. A2);
Μὴν Ἀξιοττηνὸς ἐξ Ἐπικράτου (nos. 31, 37)
Μὴν ἐγ Διοδότου (no. 66 — all of these instances are from Lydia). This question was firmly settled by Keil and von Premerstein in 1911[2] and has never been reopened. The accumulation of evidence since their time has added further support to their conclusions that thus the founders of local shrines or cult associations are immortalized.

The same would seem to hold true of Μὴν Φαρνάκου known only from Strabo[3] as a god who had a rich temple in Pontus, and by whom the Pontic kings swore the royal oath. Drexler seems quite right[4] in saying that this name must indicate the alleged founding of the temple by Pharnaces, husband of Cyrus' aunt Atossa, and legendary founder of the Pontic and Cappadocian dynasties.[5]

---

[1] The phenomenon of epithets in the genitive is not restricted to Men-cult. Cf. Josef Keil, "Zeus Trosu," *Anzeiger Akad. Wien, Phil.-Hist. Klasse*, 87, 1950, 83 ff.; Herrmann and Polatkan, *Das Testament des Epikrates*, no. 15. See also what was said above about Zeus Ariou, p. 24, n. 30, and p. 38, n. 77.

[2] *Zweite Reise*, p. 104.

[3] XII, iii, 31 (= T. 1).

[4] Roscher's *Lexikon*, s.v. Men, col. 2752.

[5] I have pointed out elsewhere (*Berytus*, 17, 1967-8, p. 94 ff.) that the Persian element is likely to have been very strong in the origin of the cult of Men. This argument was based on the iconographic resemblance between Men and Mao (as illustrated on the coins of Kanishka and Huvishka), as well as on the frequent association between Men and the indisputably Persian

More trouble attaches to the names Μὴν Κάρου (known only from Strabo, T. 3, and coin Attouda 1) and Μὴν Τιάμου (recorded in nos. 34, 35, 43, 45, 49, 51, 53, 57, 59, 60, 63, 73, 74, and 82, all from Lydia). In the first case we can still do no better than Keil and von Premerstein's suggestion,[6] "bei Karos wäre der Gedanke an einem mythischen Eponymen des karischen Stammes nicht ausgeschlossen."[7] At all events, although we may have trouble finding the name among real people, I do not think that there can be any doubt but that it was conceived of as a genitive, referring to the founder of the sanctuary.

Men Tiamou is stickier. Again, I do not think there can be any doubt as to the fact that the name was thought by the worshippers to be a genitive of a proper name,[8] even though the name Τίαμος seems only once to be recorded, by Ramsay from Isauria, and at that questionably.[9]

This name, like Λαβάνας and Καμαρείτης, which we will discuss later, has been subjected to what can be called the *interpretatio Semitica*. The resemblance to the name of the well-known Assyro-Babylonian goddess Tiamat is of course striking. Perhaps the strongest proponent of the *interpretatio Semitica* has been J. H. Wright.[10] Since Tiamat is a divinity of the underground waters, he sets up the equation *Tiamou = katachtonios*.[11]

Anahita. The matter of Men Pharnakou, although not considered at that point, merely strengthens the argument.

[6] *Zweite Reise, loc. cit.*

[7] Possibly even the Roman name Carus should be considered, in view of the evident Romanization of the cult elsewhere.

[8] Cf. A. D. Nock, *Essays on Religion and the Ancient World*, Cambridge, Mass., 1972, I, p. 156, note 112.

[9] *JHS*, 25, 1905, p. 173, no. 54. Drexler, *art. cit.*, col. 2753, gives up on this epithet.

[10] *Harvard Studies in Classical Philology*, 6, 1895, 68 ff.

[11] A new twist is given to this interpretation by G. Neumann (*Untersuchungen zum Weiterleben hetitischen und luwischen Sprachgutes in hellenistischer und römischer Zeit*, Wiesbaden, 1961, pp. 71-72) who keeps the meaning, but wishes to connect it with a Luwian word. Looking in this direction for *actual* etymologies is probably more fruitful than looking to the Semitic, although this one is far from proved, since it is merely an assumption in thin air that *Tiamou* means *katachthonios*. But in any case, the etymology, even if real, would still probably have been meaningless to Men's worshippers in imperial times, who understood *Tiamou* as a genitive of a proper name.

But the *interpretatio Semitica* falls down on the fact, historically, that it is impossible to put one's finger on a time when Semitic influence is known to have been so overriding in Western Anatolia as to influence the religion.[12] Besides, even if this etymology (from Tiamat) should be accepted, what has the *interpretatio Semitica* done to improve our understanding of the cult? I have argued elsewhere[13] that it is not the actuality of an etymology that is of importance for understanding a cult, so much as whether the supposed etymology could have been believed by the faithful in the second and third centuries A.D. Thus the word-resemblances suggested by *Askaenos*, *Tymoleitos*, etc., although they may prove nothing about actual kinship between Anatolians and Italians, would have been meaningful to the Anatolian population of the Imperial period, who were constantly in touch with their Roman overlords, particularly if the supposed connection was pushed as a matter of policy.

But can the word-resemblances of *Tiamou*, *Kamareites*, and *Labanas*, whether or not founded on any historical fact, be held to have meant anything to the Anatolians of the imperial period? In what circles, except perhaps Jewish ones, would matters Semitic be as well-known as matters Roman? How much would they be aware of the culture of their neighbors to the southeast, now, like themselves, a subject population? I do not think very much.[14]

Word-resemblances, by themselves, do not mean very much. We can prove by the river Potomac that the Ancient Greeks discovered America. As to the historical basis of the *interpretatio Semitica*, we must suspend judgment, although I find it unlikely that there is much historical basis. What is sure, however, is that these word-resemblances were probably not very meaningful to Men's worshippers. In short, the *interpretatio Semitica* fails to point in any

[12] I have discussed this matter already, *Berytus*, 17, 1967-8, pp. 93-94, and noted the difficulties and tenuousness of the Semitic approach.

[13] *Numen*, p. 22, 1975, p. 237.

[14] That there was Jewish influence in Anatolia is indisputable, the most remarkable evidence of it being the well-known Noah's ark coins of Apamea Kibotos. (See Kraabel, *art. cit.*, pp. 84-87, for evidence of Jewish influence.) But direct Jewish influence on Men-cult I have yet to find. Shared features such as angels and the title *kyrios* belong to a larger pool of commonly held religious ideas of the period.

helpful direction. Whereas the *interpretatio Romana* or the *interpretatio Persica* consistently elucidate aspects of what may really be held to have happened, the introduction of the cult by one ruling power and its exploitation by another, the *interpretatio Semitica* does not point to any historical likelihood. As such, I think that it is of little help in understanding the cult of Men.

We have digressed here to treat in some detail the matter of the Semitic interpretation, which we will have occasion to return to later also. Let us now turn back to our scrutiny of the various epithets. Of the second, or adjectival, category, the majority are geographical or pseudo-geographical. A good example of an unquestionably geographical epithet is Selmeenos, recorded in nos. 107 and 109. It has to be connected with the δῆμος Σελμεηνῶν, of no. 108. Others of probable geographical nature include Οὐινδιεινός (no. 153), although there we encounter dispute just what city of Vindia to connect the epithet with.[15] Other geographical epithets include Καουαληνός (no. 102) which has been used to assign this monument to a place of origin, since it has been in England since before 1800; and Δωλανός (no. A7), which can be identified with a known tribe from the area of Nicomedeia.[16]

Another which seems clearly geographical is Μοτελλείτης (nos. 39 and 41). L. Robert,[17] seems to be unduly hesitant in identifying the two variants Μοτυλείτης and Μοτελλείτης. The latter he derives from a known place, Motella, present day Medele, in the bend of the Meander. He does not, however, explain why this ethnic should be used on a stone which we have no reason to doubt originated at Gyölde.

It is surprising, however, just how many of these epithets seem to be geographical, but are not attested, to my knowledge, elsewhere

---

[15] *MAMA*, VII, pp. xviii-xix; Ramsay, *Social Basis of Roman Rule in Asia Minor*, Aberdeen, 1941, p. 152. Ramsay claims to have known about this stone in private hands as far back as 1901, something I failed to indicate in its lemma in *CMRDM*, I.

[16] Sencer Şahin, *Neufunde von antiken Inschriften in Nikomedeia (Izmit) und in der Umgebung der Stadt*, Diss. Münster, 1973, no. 35, with further references.

[17] *Nouvelles Inscriptions de Sardes*, Paris, 1964, p. 36. For a similar geographically displaced epithet, see Herrmann and Polatkan, *op. cit.*, no. 15, on Zeus Trosou.

than in Men-cult. Thus, in many cases, the names of places now entered on a map of ancient Asia Minor have been derived from these apparently geographical epithets.

Such, for example, is Cilvastianus (no. 20). Since this stone was dedicated by a soldier stationed at Sarmizegetusa, the assumption is that it represents an imported cult from some as yet unlocated place in Asia Minor.[18] An epithet with a variation of the same initial syllable is Κολιανοκωμήτης (no. 96), providing it applies to Men, and not to the dedicant. It too seems geographical but refers to an unknown place.

Τουιτηνός (no. 98) would seem to be related to the ethnic Τ(ε)υιτηνός recorded in the Tekmoreian lists, but does not seem to be connectable to any known place.[19]

Ξευναγονηνός (no. 115) recalls the name of the dedicant, Ξεῦνα, in no. 92. This is not an uncommon name, but apart from that I am unable to shed any light on the ethnic.[20]

Γοισηανός (G17) also seems to be an ethnic, but I am unable to shed any light on it either. So does 'Ανδρωνεινός (no. 157), and it was on the basis of this name that the name of the place where it was found is conjectured to be Androna.

Occasionally, these ethnics appear in the genitive plural, thus recalling our first category. Such are Τοληςέων (no. 103) and Πλουριστρέων (no. 127). In the first instance I have come across no parallel.[21] In the latter case, we again have confirmation from the Tekmorean lists, where Πλουριστρεύς occurs.[22]

[18] For names beginning Κιλ-, see L. Robert, *Noms Indigènes dans l'Asie Mineure Gréco-Romaine*, Paris, 1963, p. 400, note 4. In A8 we have Ζεὺς Κιλλαμενηνός. The evidence for this inscription does not point to any particular place. Perhaps to be connected are the Kilbianoi of the Upper Cayster Valley near Keles. See Keil and von Premerstein, *Bericht über eine dritte Reise in Lydien, Denkschriften Akad. Wien, Phil.-Hist. Klasse*, 57, i, 1914, p. 56 ff. See E. Schwertheim, *Istanbuler Mitteilungen*, 25, 1975, p. 358, for these names.

[19] W. M. Ramsay, *Studies in the History and Art of the Eastern Provinces of the Roman Empire*, Aberdeen, 1906, p. 323, 2, 65; p. 325, 2, 84; p. 337, 15, 44.

[20] Instances of the name are collected *MAMA*, V, p. 9.

[21] Perhaps it is to be connected with Tlos. Cf. Stephanus of Byzantium, *s.v.*, ἔστι καὶ ἄλλη Τλώς, πόλις Πισιδίας. Ramsay thinks the ethnic Τλουηνός in the Tekmoreian lists may come from this same second Tlos.

[22] Ramsay, *Studies*, p. 322, 2, 237; p. 342, 19, 17.

Finally, before we leave this discussion of fairly certain geographical names for those that are pseudo-geographical, let us observe that in one case we have an incomplete name that fits this category: ...πυκηνός (no. 111). Furthermore, Πατάλαος (A9) the most recent addition to the roster of Men's epithets, is also probably to be viewed as geographical, but it is striking that the epithet is not that of the *demos* to whom the statue of Men is dedicated.

The pseudo-geographical epithets I have had occasion to mention previously in other connections, but they should still be reviewed here. They are such as Τυμωλεῖτος (or -ης) in no. 81. This is, at first glance, purely geographical, and refers to the known Lydian community of the Τυμωλεῖται.[23] I have pointed out elsewhere, however,[24] that this epithet, although connectable with a known place, was used because of overtones which it has and which connected it with Italy and with the assumed Italian-Anatolian relationship.

Much the same can be said for *Askaenos*, the most widespread of all epithets for Men. Although in nos. 162-163, this epithet is connected with a place-name, 'Ασκαίη, I am of the opinion that this place is really fictional, or better, a sort of poetic name for all of Asia Minor. I have pointed out[25] that this name was used to underscore the supposed Anatolian-Italian kinship, and that it is no accident that it was particularly used in the Roman colony of Antioch.[26] This tendency reaches its apogee in the title *Italikos* of no. 93.

Although the Italian connection is not present, the same remarks can be made about *Axiottenos*, the second-commonest of Men's epithets.[27] Although "Αξιττα or 'Αξίοττα appears as a place-name

[23] *Sardis*, VII, i, no. 152, with references to further bibliography.
[24] *Numen*, 22, 1975, p. 238.
[25] *Art. cit.* p. 235-236.
[26] G. Neumann, *op. cit.*, p. 44 ff., following in the footsteps of W. M. Calder, who wants to see a specific local application for *Askaie*, wishes to connect it with the Hittite word *Aska*, "gate" by extension, "place of justice." He is however, embarrassed by the extensive use of the word in other parts of Asia Minor. Be it as it may with this as an actual etymology, the same remarks I have made on the subject of *Tiamou* hold true here also: the etymology would have meant nothing to the Roman-period worshipper, and the Romans would have been free to exploit the term as they found fit.
[27] See above, p. 32.

in nos. 43, 44, 86, and A1, I would be surprised should it ever be possible to pin down a place with that as its normal, legal name. Rather it seems that we are probably dealing with a sacred or poetic name for a wide area of Lydia.

Gallikos (no. 90) is more troublesome. So much so that Buckler[28] wished to reject it and substitute a feminine proper name Γαλλικώ.[29] Since the discovery of Men Italikos, however, Men Gallikos has been restored to genuinity, I think. As so often, the mysterious evidence for this cult has to be taken at face value, and flies in the face of plausible rationalization. I would like to suggest that the most profitable line of investigation here would be in the direction of the Γάλλοι (priests of Cybele), Γαλάται (Galatians), and the river-name Γάλλος, applied to several rivers in Asia Minor.[30]

Whether there was any connection originally between the name of the rivers and that of the priests, on the one hand,[31] and that of the Galatians, on the other, or whether, as is more likely, this is a coincidence which was later exploited, just as similarities of name between Anatolia and Italy were exploited, the great shrine of the Cybele-Attis cult fell early enough into Galatian hands.[32] The propagandistic purposes are great and obvious. Secondly, the similarities between Men and Attis, iconographically at least, go very far back, and are not restricted to the Attis Menotyrannus inscriptions. Men is present on coins of Pessinus from an early date. The Men-plate from Hildesheim, generally called the Attis-plate, is supposedly of Augustan date. Men also appears on the coinage of the Galatian king Deiotarus, as well as of the *koinon* of the Galatians.[33] I would like therefore to suggest that the epithet Men Gallikos can therefore be understood very well if one takes it as an attempt to draw Men into the Galatian-Pessinuntine circle. This

---

[28] *ABSA*, 21, 1914-16, p. 182.
[29] For Γαλλικός as a proper name, see *MAMA*, I, p. 32.
[30] *RE*, s.v., *Gallos*, nos. 1-4.
[31] See particularly Cumont in *RE*, s.v. *Gallos*, no. 5.
[32] In 163 B.C., a letter from King Eumenes to Attis, high-priest at Pessinus (*OGIS*, 315) shows this Attis to be Galatian — he has a brother named Aiorix. For what it is worth, there is a Gallic Attis recorded by Polybius, II, 21, 5, in Italy in 236 B.C.
[33] *CMRDM*, II, p. 151 ff.

line of propaganda, however, seems to have been less exploited than the Italian one.

Of the adjectival epithets for Men that are not obviously geographical or pseudo-geographical, most are words with straightforward Greek meanings. The three that do not fit either of these categories are Λαβάνας, Πετραείτης, and Καμαρείτης. They thus call for special discussion.

Λαβάνας is recorded only in two inscriptions (nos. 42 and 62), both of the Kula-area. We are in no better position to elucidate this name now than was Drexler, over seventy years ago, who comes to the conclusion that it is probably geographical.[34] To use our terminology, we might say, "pseudo-geographical." Drexler calls it "verführerisch" to attempt to connect it with the Hebrew *laban*, "white." I have already discussed the fruitlessness of the *interpretatio Semitica*; the geographical surmises which have been made are likewise only stabs in the dark.[35]

Πετραείτης is known from four inscriptions (nos. 34, 62, 67, and 68), again, all from the Kula area. Going by the ending, one would conclude that we are here dealing with a geographical epithet. Parallels for the formation are provided by *Motelleites* and *Tymoleites* (if that, not *Tymoleitos*, is the proper form of the nominative), both of which seem, at least on the surface level, seem to refer to actual places. Another parallel in formation is provided by Apollo Nisyreites, whose cult is known to go back to the second century B.C. and whose name is clearly connected with a Νισυρέων κατοικία.[36]

We do not know, however, of any community with which *Petraeites* can be matched.[37] The possibility of its being pseudo-geo-

[34] *Art. cit.*, col. 2750.
[35] All such conjectures up to their own time were assembled by Keil and von Premerstein, *Zweite Reise*, p. 103, and to my knowledge, there have been none since. They include the Carian Λάβαρα, or else Ἀλάβανδα. Also a land on the Black Sea, known from Assyrian sources.
[36] For the god: *AM*, 1892, p. 198, no. 1; Keil and von Premerstein, *Zweite Reise*, nos. 199, 202, 203; Herrmann, no. 28 is dated in the second year of King Attalus, *i.e.*, 158-7 or 138-7 B.C. For the community, see Keil and von Premerstein, *op. cit.*, nos. 192 and 200.
[37] The closest which Drexler can adduce is from an inscription of Telmessos.

graphical cannot be ruled out, but it is not clear in what direction this would point, as it is in the cases of *Askaenos, Gallikos,* or even *Axiottenos*. An obvious suggestion is to connect it with "rock," but the meaning would remain unclear. Apart from the Attis Menotyrannus inscriptions, Men has no particular relation to the rockborn Mithras, only once (no. 21) borrowing an epithet which commonly is applied to him. We must leave our judgment suspended.

Likewise in the case of *Kamareites* (recorded in nos. 55 (?), 56, Nysa coins 4 and 5, and the monument mentioned by L. Robert)[38] we must confess ourselves pretty much in the dark. Although this epithet is not restricted to the Lydian area, as are the two previously discussed, there are still no good hints to go on. The only two conjectures so far made were already known to Drexler, 1) that the name is connected with *qamar*, "moon" in Arabic. This would not only be redundant, but again shows the unhelpfulness of the *interpretatio Semitica*, which has so far pointed to a Babylonian goddess, a Hebrew adjective, and an Arabic noun. 2) The other suggestion has been that of connecting it with καμάρα, which is frequently used in Asia Minor to mean "grave."[39] Thus *Men Kamareites* would mean much the same thing as *Men Katachthonios*. The obvious objection is that the name nowhere appears in a funerary context. This fact may be mitigated somewhat, however, by the fact that on other coins of Nysa the underworld divinities are very prominent: Pluto, Kore, the rape of Kore, Zeus Ploutodotes.[40]

Likewise the vegetation-aspect of the underworld gods is emphasized — the ear of grain is called punningly κόρος ("satiety" or masculine for Κόρη).[41] In this context, it seems possible to make some sense, then, of *Men Kamareites*, even if we cannot arrive at sure conclusions. In particular, in spite of all the argumentation given above, the ending of the adjective continues to look more like a geographical or pseudo-geographical formation.

Turning now to the epithets applied to Men which have obvious meaning in Greek, one finds that the dividing line between them and

[38] *Laodicée du Lycos, Le Nymphée*, Quebec and Paris, 1969, p. 289, n. 5.
[39] See Kubinska, *op. cit.*, p. 94 ff.
[40] Cf. Men's title on our no. 142.
[41] See Regling, in *Nysa ad Mäandrum*, Deutsches Archäologisches Institut, Jahrbuch, Ergänzungsheft 10, 1913, p. 91 ff.

the simple adjectives expressing aspects of the god's power is virtually impossible to make. One of the commonest and most characteristic titles for Men, which so far as I know does not occur in any other cult, is *Tyrannos*.[42] Its geographical distribution is scattered: 11-13 (Attica), 15 (Thasos), 30 (Pergamum), 36, 53, 61, A8 (Lydia). It also gives rise in the fourth century to the syncretistic combination Attis Menotyrannus, known from Italy (nos. 22-27; AD2-AD4), from a magical papyrus,[43] and perhaps at an earlier date from Serdica (no. D3).

The meaning seems clear. It expresses the absolute authority of Men over all aspects of the life of the worshipper.[44] As such, it is not surprising to find it primarily in the Lydian material, where, as we have already observed, the texts are pervaded with a sense of the god's great powers for good or for ill.[45] Nor is it surprising to find this title absent in central Anatolia and at Antioch, where Men-worship seems to be a more public, formal thing. The surprise is really that it is not even more widespread in the material from Lydia, given the appropriateness with which it expresses the religious outlook of that area.[46]

Ouranios is probably the most obvious of all possible epithets for the divinity of a heavenly body, and needs no explanation. Its geographical distribution is wide, but thin: 7 (Attica), 32, 83 (Lydia), 92, 94, 95 (region of Dorylaeum), 129 (Pisidia), 156 and A5 (Lycaonian and Cilician grave imprecations). In the last two instances it is associated, probably for contrast, with Men Katachthonios.[47]

Katachthonios, on the other hand, is definitely limited in its geographical range. The inscriptions in which it occurs (143-150, 156, A5 and AD5 — if indeed this inscription with its multiple Mens can

---

[42] It is admittedly borrowed by Zeus in our no. 54, but according to Bömer, *op. cit.*, p. 204 (= 446), this is a unique occurrence.

[43] *Papyri Graecae Magicae*, ed. K. Preisendanz, et al., Leipzig, 1928, p. 156, line 2664. Actually, in the papyrus as it should be emended, Selene is being addressed as μόνη τύραννε but in the papyrus as it stands we have Μηνοτύραννε and the corruption in the text certainly seems to have occurred under the influence of the epithet of Attis.

[44] Bömer, *op. cit.*, p. 441 (= 199) Steinleitner, *op. cit.*, p. 82.

[45] See above, in the chapter on *The Cult in Lydia*.

[46] See particularly above, pp. 32-33.

[47] Cf. also Helios Plouton in our inscription no. 28.

have anything to do with the cult as normally conceived) are all sepulchral monuments of the Lycaonian-Cilician area. Once it occurs in the variant *chthonios* (no. 151) from the same area. It cannot be said that the name, or the function of protecting graves (which also occurs in Lydia, nos. 70 and 71) is particularly obvious for a lunar divinity. (As we said above, however, there is a possibility that *Men Kamareites* points in the same direction.) Θεοὶ καταχθόνιοι are of course well known without specification.[48] The psychological connection with the moon seems to be via the idea of darkness,[49] but scholars have had to grope around in cultures far removed from that of Roman Asia Minor to find parallels. The goddess Hecate provides a sort of parallel in functions; she is occasionally associated with Men (nos. 89, 99, cf. 118) but significantly not in this group of material. The idea of the moon as resting place of souls, common in late paganism and brilliantly expounded by F. Cumont,[50] may have some bearing, if indirectly. Still none of this really suffices to explain this peculiar, local belief, which may go back to ideas prevalent in the region before the advent of Greco-Roman culture, and about which we have no records.

Patrios is restricted to Antioch in Pisidia — agonistic inscriptions (164-174) and dedications (177, 263, 270, 288, 290). As we observed in our chapter on Antioch, this usage reflects not only the real antiquity of the Men-cult there, but the apparent effort of the Romans to promote the cult in their colony for propagandistic purposes.

Σωτὴρ καὶ Πλουτοδώτης is recorded only on the amazing syncretistic relief, no. 142. We have had occasion already to compare this with the same usage in the cult of Sarapis, and will expand on the subject later, in the chapter on iconography.[51]

[48] See the article *Katachthonioi* in Roscher's *Lexikon*, II, i, col. 998 ff., to say nothing of more recent material; once in our context, no. 147, Θεοὶ καταχθόνιοι appear; there are also various other gods, such as Zeus, Pluto, Demeter, Persephone, and the Furies, who specifically bear the title.

[49] *Art. cit.*, cols. 999-1000.

[50] In his chapter, "La Lune Séjour des Morts," in *Recherches sur le Symbolisme Funéraire des Romains*, Paris, 1942. See also C. Préaux, *La lune dans la pensée grecque*, Mem. Ac. Royale Belg., Ser. 2, 61, iv, 1973, esp. pp. 135-144.

[51] Cf. also the use of σωτηρία, etc., in nos. 41, 72, 88, 91, 92, 105, 107, and A6, as well as the use of Zeus Ploutodotes on coins of Nysa.

Ἀνείκητος occurs only once, in an inscription of Dacia, if indeed it is correctly read.[52] It was placed there by a soldier, and under the circumstances, it is not surprising that Men borrowed from Mithras or from the unconquered Sun so appropriately military an epithet. It should be noted, however, that only in nos. 20 and 21, both from Dacia, does Men appear as a soldier's god. It is not one of his normal functions.

Φωσφόρος, recorded of Men only in the dice-oracles, 132-136, and thus probably devoid of cult significance, is an obvious epithet for a moon-god.

In the fragmentary no. 52, Men appears to be called ὅσιος and in no. 88, he is called ὅσιος καὶ δίκαιος. This combination of adjectives is common, both as a divinity in itself (sometimes occuring in the feminine or in the plural) and as an epithet for the θεῖον or for an angel.[53]

In no. 130, Men is called ἐπιφανής, something which is entirely appropriate in view of the epiphanies on the Attic reliefs, the ἴχνη of no. 85, and the general habit of this god to communicate directly with the worshipper, not through intermediaries.[54]

Ἐπήκοος is an adjective frequently applied — nos. 46 (?), Lydia; 104, 124, 125 (central Anatolia); 280, 285 (Antioch). Again, for a god whose answering of prayers seems to be so frequent and so efficacious, the epithet is not surprising. The adjective is by no means limited to Men. It is particularly common in the cult of Sarapis.[55] To name only a few other instances, in Pisidia it is applied

---

[52] An examination of the line-drawing given in *CMRDM*, I, should convince the reader that we cannot have too much confidence in this inscription.

[53] See L. Robert, *Anatolia*, 3, 1958, 117 ff. = *Opera Minora Selecta*, I, 416 ff., with extensive further references; as far as I know the promised monograph on this cult has never appeared. See also Herrmann and Polatkan, *Das Testament des Epikrates*, p. 49 ff.; interestingly, in no. 9, p. 51 ὅσιος καὶ δίκαιος is combined with εἷς καὶ μόνος θεός, which will be discussed below.

[54] Again, a good discussion and listing of parallels is given by L. Robert, *Anatolia*, 3, 1958, 112 ff. = *Opera Minora Selecta*, I, 411 ff.; *Hellenica*, 6, 1948, p. 51, and references.

[55] Vidman, *SIRIS*, 287, 381, 389, 788. For Artemis Anaeitis ἐπήκοος, see Robert, *Hellenica*, 6, 1948, p. 109. Weinreich, *AM*, 37, 1912, pp. 1-68, has an abundant collection of the earlier material, including many reliefs which include representations of the god's ears.

to Artemis, Pluto and Kore, and Asclepius.[56]

If we can trust Calder's reading of our no. 155,[57] the multiple Mens of that inscription are called ἀνεπίλυτοι. The adjective is rare; Liddell-Scott-Jones give only two examples, in one of which it means "unbandaged," and in the other "unsolved."[58] Neither meaning is appropriate for us. The meaning can only be that of the ineluctability of the curse; we may compare it with the phrases λυθῆναι τὸ σκῆπτρον, ἔλοισε τοὺς ὅρκους of nos. 44 and 51.

One of the most striking praises of Men is to be found in no. 83, from Saittae, a place where the Men-cult is also well-attested numismatically: Εἷς θεὸς ἐν οὐρανοῖς, μέγας Μὴν Οὐράνιος, μεγάλη δύναμις τοῦ ἀθανάτου θεοῦ.

The emphasis on μέγας is not unusual. We have it also in nos. 42, 43, 51, 67, and 69, all from Lydia. It is common also in the Sarapis-cult.[59] Aelius Aristides shouts: μέγας ὁ 'Ασκληπιός.[60] The best known example to the general public is, "Great is Artemis of the Ephesians."[61]

Nor is the emphasis on the *power* of the god unusual, being commonplace in the Lydian inscriptions.[62] More striking is εἷς θεός, as it appears at first glance to be a claim for total monotheism. Yet, although isolated in Men-cult, this phenomenon is not isolated in late paganism. It too grows from an acclamation, as Peterson clearly points out.[63] The tri-partite nature of the formula in our inscription is such as to make this evident.

Again, parallels are present from Sarapis-cult — the well-known acclamation εἷς Ζεὺς Σάραπις.[64] One is reminded also of a passage

[56] SEG, 19, nos. 802, 827, and 853. See also the dedication of ἴχνη, above, p. 25.
[57] See CMRDM, II, p. 178.
[58] L. Robert, *Hellenica*, 13, makes no comment on this word while discussing these inscriptions.
[59] Vidman, SIRIS, index, s.vv., Σάραπις μέγας, θεὸς μέγας Σάραπις, Ζεὺς μέγας Σάραπις. Ζεὺς μέγας Σάραπις Ἥλιος. I have not seen B. Müller, Μέγας Θεός, *Dissertationes philologicae Halenses*, 21, 1913, 317 ff.
[60] Ἱεροὶ Λόγοι, II, 7.
[61] *Acts*, 19, 28. For this acclamation in general, see Peterson, Εἷς Θεός, Göttingen, 1926, p. 200 ff.
[62] Nos. 43, 44, 51, 53, 62, 63, 67, and A1.
[63] *Op. cit.*, p. 269. See also L. Robert, *Anatolia*, 3, 1958, 128 ff. = *Opera Minora Selecta*, I, 427 ff.
[64] Vidman, SIRIS, nos. 363, 389, and 679. In the last case, admittedly,

in Aelius Aristides:[65] Κἀγὼ περιχαρὴς τῇ τιμῇ γενόμενος καὶ ὅσον τῶν ἄλλων προὐκρίθην, ἐξεβόησα, "εἷς," λέγων δὴ τὸν θεόν. Καὶ ὃς ἔφη, "σὺ εἶ."

It is just such transports of pagan religious enthusiasm as were experienced by the remarkable Aelius Aristides from which one can imagine this praise of Men to have arisen. It is unnecessary to see Jewish influence, or any other consistent monotheism.

there is Jewish influence, but the rest are purely pagan.

[65] Ἱεροὶ Λόγοι, IV, 50.

CHAPTER SIX

ASSOCIATIONS OF MEN WITH OTHER DIVINITIES

As well as looking at the adjectives and other epithets applied to the god, in order to determine what the worshippers thought of him, it should be possible also to derive information from Men's association with other gods. In particular, the theory repeated almost *ad nauseam* about "Anatolian" religions, is that they center on a mother goddess and her young consort, of which Cybele and Attis are always taken as the prototype. It should be interesting, with the material which we have gathered here, to see to what extent this generality agrees with the reality of the cult, as revealed by our study.

In a number of the Lydian inscriptions, Men is invoked together with a mother goddess. In no. 34, she is not identified with any epithet in the preserved part of the inscription (Ταζηνῆς would fit), whereas in nos. 42 and 67, she is called Μήτηρ Ταζηνή and in no. 47 Μήτηρ Ταρσηνή, probably another form of the same name. In no. 84, Men is associated with Μήτηρ Πλαστήνη, insofar as a statue of him was dedicated to her.[1] The interesting monument no. A8 calls the figure (Cybele by iconography) standing next to Men in the relief field, by the name τεκοῦσα,[2] and the implication, although the grammar is none too clear, is that she is thought of as being Men's *mother*. This very interesting inscription, then, is our only indication as to how relationships were conceived of among these gods, and it is one that has striking parallelism to Christianity, which Men-cult was competing with. Also one should mention that among the gods associated with Men in the joint priesthoods of no. 101 was Μήτηρ Ἀγδιστις.

It is, of course, an error in methodology to attach too much

[1] But this is a fairly slim connection, as no. 34 shows a statue of Dionysus dedicated to Men and a mother goddess, and no. 89, apparently shows a dedication of a statue of Asclepius to Men and Hecate. In addition, statues of Men or dedications to him in temples of other gods are fairly numerous — *e.g.*, nos. 8 (from a Metroon), 18, 19, and 28.

[2] Unfortunately misaccented even in the final version of *CMRDM*, II.

importance to the exceptional, rather than the normal, and unfortunately inscription no. A8 has not been provided with any parallels as yet. It may be remarked, however, that it provides a context for the hitherto unexplained baby-Men of no. 64, if we now know that Men has a mother. But granted the sameness of so much of the material on Men, we are justified in grabbing onto the one deviant piece of evidence which tells us something that the others may simply be assuming. At all events, we may be grateful to the inscription at least for indicating to us that that relationship between Men and the figure shown next to him is conceived of as a mother-son relationship, whatever relationship (if any) may be assumed to underlie the other associations of Men with a female divinity.

We thus have, in addition to a great deal of silence, one piece of information which points to Men's being the son of an (unnamed) associated goddess, as opposed to no information (except indirectly, through syncretism with Attis) of his being considered that goddess's male consort. It is of course tantalizing that the goddess remains here unidentified except as Men's mother. Is she Meter Tazene? A representation of this goddess[3] shows her iconographically as a typical Cybele-type. Is she Artemis Anaeitis, whom we will discuss next? Coins of Hypaipa and Hierocaesarea, where Artemis Anaeitis was especially worshipped, show her as the Ephesian type, and as a huntress, respectively, but a monument described but not illustrated by Buresch[4] seems to show an Artemis as a typical Cybele type. What could this monument tell us about an unknown local mythology? Or about local variations on standard Persian or Greek mythology? Unfortunately, the questions can only be posed, not answered, in the present state of our evidence.

A complicated situation is posed by the Artemis Anaeitis group of associated female divinities, which show overlap with the mother-goddess group. In nos. 35, 45, 60, and 71, she is referred to as Ἀνάειτις or θεὰ Ἀνάειτις, and in no. 43 as Μήτηρ Ἀνάειτις. In nos. 44,

[3] *Musée Belge*, 11, 1907, p. 134. The reference from Suidas, T. 12, would seem at first glace to connect Men with a mother-goddess, but probably rests on confusion of Μητραγύρτης with Μηναγύρτης as does the variation in the name of Antiphanes' play.

[4] *Aus Lydien*, p. 69.

57, 59, 63, and 74, Artemis has joined the syncretism, and we have ῎Αρτεμις ᾿Ανάειτις whereas in nos. 49 and 51, Anaeitis has dropped out and we have Μήτηρ ῎Ατιμις, which, for lack of a better explanation, I can only regard as a variant of Artemis.

Now Anaeitis is well known from literary sources to have been introduced into Asia Minor and to have become associated with Artemis — a particular center of worship was Hierocaesareia.[5] As appears from the remarks above, we do not really know how the goddess would have been represented, but it remains a reasonable guess that in the Maeonian area she might have been normally shown more or less like the τεκοῦσα-figure of no. A8. This connection with Anaeitis is of course one of the strongest arguments for seeing a Persian connection for Men.[6]

Coins of Saittae, nos. 10, 13, and 14, very close geographically to the Kula-area, show Men standing in front of a seated Cybele-type. Again, the goddess is nowhere given a name, but it would seem reasonable to associate her with Meter Tazene, and perhaps the Artemis Anaeitis group.

In no. 75, Men is associated with Demeter in mysteries. These mysteries are unique in Men-cult, and it hardly needs pointing out that Demeter is the mystery-goddess *par excellence*. Probability dictates that Men has somehow here become stuck onto some local Lydian ceremonial which aspires to be an imitator of the great mysteries at Eleusis.

But Men's association with Demeter does not end here. Our coin, Silandus 3, likewise Lydian, shows a goddess with grain and poppy, and this representation has traditionally been taken as that of Demeter, goddess of the earth's fertility. Likewise it is not perhaps entirely by accident that the priesthoods of Men and Demeter are joined in the person who presided over the games held at Antioch in Pisidia about 300 A.D. (161, 164-174).

Other connections of Men with female divinities are more remote and tell us less about this divinity. It is clear, for instance, that

---

[5] The literary references are conveniently collected in Roscher's *Lexikon*, I, i, s.v., *Artemis*, col. 332. The material which we are handling here shows that the cult had a greater geographic range than is indicated by that article.

[6] I have discussed this matter *Berytus*, 17, 1967-68, p. 94 ff. and *Aufstieg und Niedergang der römischen Welt*.

there was no conflict between Men-cult and that of the Egyptian divinities, Isis and Sarapis. We have already had several occasions to mention similarities between Men- and Sarapis-cult, such as the use of the god's footprints, or the shared titles of no. 142. In no.7, a priest of Isis and Sarapis makes a dedication to Men, and in no. 101, priesthoods of Men Askaenos and Isis are held jointly by the same person. One thus has the distinct impression, from what little evidence there is, that Men-cult and that of the Egyptian gods co-existed amicably and in close proximity, particularly in those areas (Attica and Delos, 7, 18-19) where Men-cult was not predominant, but seems to have followed in the wake of a more aggressive foreign religion.

Hecate, another goddess widely worshipped in Asia Minor,[7] is associated with Men in a number of monuments. Although not too much importance can be attached to no. 118, which records that a priest of Men Askaenos had as ancestor a priest of Hecate at Aphrodisias, nos. 89 and 99 attest a closer relationship. Hecate, also, it should be remembered, is a goddess of darkness and night, and this fits in well with the idea of Men Katachthonios. For all the difficulties involved, the most reasonable interpretation of no. 89 sees in it a dedication of a statue of Asclepius to Hecate and Men, who must therefore have been worshipped together at the same shrine.[8] No. 99, a combination dedication and grave-stele, mentions only Hecate Soteira, under whose protection Apsion placed the tomb of her husband Gaius, but the remarkable relief in the field over the portraits of the two deceased, whatever one may make of all the iconographical details, seems clearly to establish a close connection between Hecate and Men. The palm-branch, an unusual attribute which Men here holds in his hand, may have been intended for a symbol of victory, even over death, and indeed his whole costume seems to be somewhat military (a point to which we shall return in

[7] See most recently Wm. Berg in *Numen*, 21, 1974, 128 ff.

[8] Asclepius is himself, as every reader of Aelius Aristides knows, not an inconsiderable divinity in Asia Minor, but only here does he seem to be associated with Men, unless one is inclined to see a symbol of Asclepius in the staff of Magnesia coins 1-4. In view of the association of Men with medicine, attested by Strabo, T. 3, it is perhaps odd that connections with Asclepius are not more common.

the chapter on iconography), but it would be unwise, I think, to press this point too far in the absence of more specific evidence. In general, the presence of Men on a funerary stele reminds us of the Lydian/Lycaonian material, and particularly of no. 153, which is likewise apparently dedicatory and funerary.[9]

Most other associations of Men with female divinities are so remote as to be trivial. No particular significance can, I think, be ascribed to the fact that statues of both Artemis and Men are among the furniture of Helios Apollo Kisauloddenos (no. 28), that the same man holds a joint priesthood of Men and the vague abstraction Sebaste Eirene (Pax Augusta) in no. 101, or the appearance of Men with various female divinities on alliance coins: on the alliance coin of Sagalassus and Side, he represents the first city, and Athena the second, just as he represents Nysa, to Ephesian Artemis for Ephesus and Ares (perhaps Zeus, too) for Sparta.[10] On the alliance coins of Bagis and Temenothyrae, where he is shown facing Tyche, it is impossible to tell which city he is representing, being equally favored in both, but this problem seems better solved from an iconographical point of view in the analogous case of the alliance coins of Sebaste and Temenothyrae, on which the Tyches of the two cities get together to boost Men.[11]

Now I am well aware of F. Brommer's *caveat*[12] about attaching too much importance to numismatic representations, but what it seems we *can* draw from these cases in which Men represents a city on an alliance coin, or appears with the Tyche of a city, is that Men is regarded as the tutelary divinity, or one of the tutelary divinities, of the city. This feeling is borne out by Nysa, coins 19, 21, (?), 22,

---

[9] The best discussion of this and similar Hecate reliefs, but without Men, is to be found in Keil and von Premerstein, *Zweite Reise*, p. 141 ff. The double axe held by the naked figure in the relief is reminiscent of Apollo Tarsios and the other local Apollos of Asia Minor.

[10] Sagalassus and Side, *CMRDM*, II, p. 127; Nysa alliances, *CMRDM*, II, pp. 33-34. It is to be hoped that a better-preserved specimen of Nysa 43 will some time show up and resolve doubts for us.

[11] Alliance coins of Bagis and Temenothyrae, *CMRDM*, II, p. 15; of Sebaste and Temenothyrae, *ibid.*, pp. 74-75.

[12] *Chiron*, 2, 1972, p. 536, *à propos* of coins of Asia Minor with representations of Hephaistos: "Weder belegt jede Göttermünze einen Kult, noch ist jeder Kult durch eine Göttermünze belegt."

35, 36, and 40, on which the Tyche of Nysa is shown holding a statuette of Men. We can thus conclude, in spite of the silence of the epigraphical sources, that Men was probably one of the most important divinities worshipped at Nysa.[13] At Antioch in Pisidia also, where the epigraphical evidence is nothing if not abundant, the impression it gives is confirmed by coin no. 57, where Men (shown in the Antiochene type) extends his hand to the Tyche of the city. It might be possible to see in this coin a symbolized union of the city proper with the temple just outside of it, but I see no point in trying really to distinguish between the two, as Men occurs so abundantly on the indisputably municipal coinage. Indeed, unless we are to see it in just a stupid slip of the die-engraver, the inscription of Antioch 48, *Fortuna Col. Antioch.*, could even be taken as meaning that the engraver saw only an outward difference, not a difference in meaning, between the Men-reverse and the equally common Fortuna (Tyche) reverse on the coins of Antioch — he was thus unconcerned which name he gave to which representation.

The relationship between Men and the moon-goddess Selene, on the other hand, is more difficult to handle. One must first ask oneself whether the sex of the divinity was all that important a consideration in the eyes of the worshipper, or whether (as seems more likely) there were certain moon-functions which one could reasonably expect any moon-divinity to carry out, regardless of sex. Sex thus is reduced to a consideration of secondary importance, to be assigned rather arbitrarily to the divinity as the accidents of name and grammatical gender happen to dictate. (This I think is the right interpretation of Strabo, XII, iii, 31 = T. 1. Men is simply being called Selene, and Strabo is not implying that there were both male and female moon divinities in Pontus. The same conclusion is to be drawn from the passage of Clement of Alexandria, TD1.)

We can start, I think, by excluding from consideration such monuments as no. 100, where counterbalancing busts of Helios and Selene are located above a central pedimental area containing the

---

[13] K. Regling goes so far, in his "Überblick über die Münzen von Nysa," in *JDAI*, Ergänzungsheft 10, to claim for Nysa the imperial cistophorus with representation of Men, *CMRDM*, II, p. 163. One should also note the connection of Men and Tyche in Strabo = T. 1.

bust of Men; such representations are too banal and familiar from, for example, Mithraic reliefs, to attract our attention. The same holds for Πλούτων Ἥλιος and Κούρη Σελήνη (in spite of their odd chthonian function) in 28, lines 20-21, whose connection with Men in the temple of Apollo Kisauloddenos is entirely coincidental.

What does one make, however, of the representation on the coins of Siblia? Certainly the Severan period coins, nos. 4 and 5, have a distinctly female appearance, and L. Robert even holds them to be Selene.[14] Yet there can be no question but that Selene, if such she is, is here represented with the attributes of the Men-type of Antioch, and that type is known to be derived from a cult-statue of the male god. The Romans in Antioch seem to have been thrown, at least temporarily, by the fact that there was no way of rendering a masculine moon-god name conveniently into their language. This, I think, accounts not only for the awkward *Mensis* of the coins (which translates the name but misses the point) and for the fact that elsewhere (mon. 178) the Romans came closer to the essence of the divinity by a defiance of grammatical gender. Thus I think that the inference is undeniable that the *dies festae Lunae* of this inscription refer simply to a feast of the god commonly called Men.

Siblia, however, is not alone in showing Men with singularly feminine features. Certain coins of Juliopolis in Bithynia (*e.g.*, 1, 4, and 6) show Men as remarkably female-looking, although, perhaps because of the concurrent presence at Juliopolis of the types of Men on horseback and Men standing, the suggestion has never to my knowledge been made that we are here dealing with a Selene.[15]

On the other hand, Men can also borrow the iconography of Selene, as is shown by the biga of bulls in which he stands on Temenothyrae coins 7, 8, 10, and 11, a type fairly obviously borrowed from or at least shared with Selene.[16]

---

[14] *Centennial Publication of the American Numismatic Society*, New York, 1958, p. 578.
[15] A similar female-looking figure which may be intended for Men is given by the plaque from the Athenian Agora, which I included as D2.
[16] Magnesia on the Maeander, *BMC, Ionia*, p. 171, no. 86 and Pl. XX, 7. Tarsus, *BMC, Lycaonia*, etc., p. 212, no. 253, and Pl. XXXVII, 3. On the coins of Tarsus, Selene, unlike Men, carries a torch, but torches are not

We have already had occasion to remark on the importance of moon-lore in general and *Men Katachthonios* in particular in beliefs concerning the tomb and the afterlife. Here likewise, the sex of the divinity seems to be a matter of little importance. Exact parallels are furnished by such divinities as *Selene Katachthonia* and Σελήνη φαίνουσα, both from Rough Cilicia.[17]

Finally, let me remark that the occasional association between Men and Pan in Attica (nos. 5 and 6) may also possibly be explained by the fact that Men and Selene are virtually one and the same thing. Although Pan-cult is attested at a number of places in Asia Minor from a fairly early (Hellenistic) date, it does not seem that any association was made between the two cults there.[18] Rather it seems to me more likely that the contact between the cults was made in Attica, and that the catalyst was the widespread connection between Pan and Selene cults, which, generally, saw Pan as enamored of Selene.[19]

But this has already led us over to our next topic, the relations between Men and various other male divinities. The most numerous associations of Men with another male divinity are with various forms of Zeus. The various Zeuses have local by-names as mysterious as those of Men, although they are at least pseudo-geographical. It does not lie within the scope of the present work to speculate on their possible origin, but it is significant that these epithets, like those in the genitive, are among the common features of several cults in Asia Minor, including Men, Zeus, and Apollo.

In the pair of votive inscriptions nos. 53-54, Men is joined with Zeus Masphalatenos. Significantly, I think, in the second of them,

unknown in Men-cult, although they seem somewhat more characteristic of Selene.

The bull in moon-lore, of course, goes back into the Iranian prehistory of these cults, and its prominence is one of the things that help convince me of the importance of the Iranian factor in them. To go into this matter in depth would, however, both be beyond my competence, and beyond the scope of this book. An interesting treatment is to be found in an article by H. Lommel, *Paideuma*, 3, 1944-49, p. 207 ff.

[17] Bean and Mitford, *Journeys in Rough Cicilia, Denkschriften Akad. Wien, Phil.-Hist. Klasse*, 102, nos. 266 and 240. Cf. also the syncretism of Selene and Persephone in our no. 28.

[18] Cf. Tuchelt, *Istanbuler Mitteilungen*, 19-20, 1969-70, 223 ff.

[19] R. Herbig, *Pan*, Frankfurt, 1949, pp. 35-36.

Zeus is called κοίριος τύραννος, both of which epithets are also applied to Men, and the significance of which we have already discussed. On the other hand, the iconographical representation of Zeus, or consistency therein, seems to be a matter of less importance. In the relief accompanying no. 54, he is portrayed as an elderly figure, resting on a staff and holding an eagle. But on no. 53, he is a young figure with the sun's rays streaming out from his head, such as would seem more appropriate for a form of Apollo. Unless we are to assume a stonemason's carelessness, or sudden reuse for another purpose of a stone originally intended for Men and Apollo, then this stone should serve as an eloquent *caveat* against excessive reliance on iconography alone in the absence of other criteria. No. 61 introduces us to the equally mysterious Zeus Ogmenos, but without giving us a picture of him. No. A8 gives us an interesting dedication *of* (not *to*) Men Tyrannos and his mother, ordered by Zeus Killamenenos[20] κατ' ἐπίπνοιαν, apparently a more graphic variant for the more normal κατ' ἐπιταγήν or κατὰ πρόσταγμα. Gem no. 13, the only gem on which a representation of Men is combined with those of other gods, shows a bust of Men, next to a representation of Hermes, one of the associated gods to be discussed below. Perhaps also to be counted among the connections of Men and a Zeus is our no. 97, where a doubtful reading would indicate a joint dedication to Men and the local Zeus Benneus of North Phrygia.[21] Finally, we should mention the fact that in no. 101 the priesthood of Men Askaenos appears *inter alia* held in common with that of Zeus Soter, thus attesting at least to a lack of enmity between the cults.

Other notable associations of Men with other male divinities include Dionysus and Sabazius. The puzzling, and apparently no longer accessible no. 15, whatever one makes of its last lines, seems to bespeak a syncretism between Men and Dionysus, and this idea seems borne out by the local representation of Men on coins of Magnesia on the Maeander, where Men appears flanked by a thyrsus and a snake-entwined staff. (The latter attribute may be referred

---

[20] It seems preferable, although not certain, to take Ἀρχελάου with κώμη, rather than with the divine name. Schwertheim, *Istanbuler Mitteilungen*, 25, 1975, pp. 358-359, comments on names like these.

[21] For this divinity, see *MAMA*, V, introduction.

either to Asclepius or to Hermes.) Lastly, in view of the evidence already amassed, particular significance, which would not accrue otherwise, may be attached to no. 34, in which a statue of Dionysus is dedicated by the καταλουστικοί of an unidentified mother, Men Tiamou, and Men Petraeites.

As to whether Sabazius and Dionysus have anything to do with one another, there is a difference of opinion, which it is not up to us to get involved in here. Basically, I would agree with Eisele[22] that as far as the relation of both divinities with Men-cult is concerned, it is not necessary to see any connection between the two of them.

The main attestation of Men-Sabazius syncretism is of course a literary reference of a later date than the cessation of Men-worship (Proclus, *In Timaeum*, IV, 251c = T. 9). Although Proclus is unlikely to have had any first-hand information on Men-cult, archaeological discoveries seem to bear out the fact that there was some basis in actuality for his statement. I think that the Sabazius-statuettes with lunar attributes, which are intended to be attached to votive hands, show that there was at least that lunar aspect to Sabazius which would make such a syncretism likely and credence is therefore to be given to Proclus' words.[23]

Hermes is also a god who is sometimes associated with Men, although I think it unwise to extract excessive conclusions from this fact. It would be attractive, for instance, to see Hermes in his guise of psychopompus and god of magic inserted into a circle which includes Men Katachthonios, Selene Katachthonia, and Hecate. Unfortunately, I do not think the evidence will take us that far. As well as the apparent caduceus on the coins of Magnesia (nos. 1-4) which point to a possible connection with Hermes, we also have the representation of Hermes on G 13, the prominence of Hermes in inscription no. 126, in his function of communicating between god and man (particularly important in this age when demonology, angelology, and the idea of a divine hierarchy are so omnipresent), and the purely formal connection of Men with Hermes Agoraios at

---

[22] Roscher's *Lexikon*, IV, col. 262, s.v. *Sabazios*.
[23] See my article in *Muse*, 8, 1974, pp. 34-37, for three such examples of Sabazius statuettes with lunar attributes. The relief of the *Koloenon katoikia*, is, however, not to the point, as it was claimed to be by Eisele.

Aphrodisias in nos. 118-120. All in all, then, connections between Men and Hermes exist, but are hardly explicit enough to allow us to base any far-reaching conclusions on them.

Another divinity with whom Men has associations is Apollo. This god appears in Asia Minor in various local forms, and one of his commonest attributes is the double axe particularly common in the Apollo Lairbenos-cult of Phrygian Hierapolis, as can be seen from the coin-representations, but also in various Lydian Apollo-cults, such as that of Apollo Tarsios, whose name may be connected with that of Meter Tarsene.[24] The only explicit joining of Men with Apollo Tarsios is in no. 47, in which Apollo Tarsios is, together with Men and Mother Tarsene, one of the gods whom Trophime asks what to do about her manic state.[25] The conjunction of gods is reflected in the appearance of both the moon-crescent and the axe above the main relief field in the stele. It is interesting, however, that the coins of Alia (nos. 5, 6, 7, and conceivably also 4) show Men riding with the double axe over his shoulder, in a very similar fashion to the various Apollos. This highly *atypical* representation of Men (in spite of what is said about its being normal in the earlier works of Ramsay, *et al.*) would seem to point to some kind of syncretism between the two concepts.

Other associations between Men and Apollo are more remote. The famous Smyrna inscription, no. 28, lists a statue of Men among the extensive cult-furniture of Helios Apollo Kisauloddenos, thus proving at least the compatibility of these two cults. In no. 92, a Phrygian dedication, Apollo is joined with Men Ouranios, and in no. 101, the priesthood of Apollo is one of a number of priesthoods held jointly with that of Men Askaenos. Finally, in no. 126, Apollo, along with other divinities, is mentioned on the same altar with Men.

[24] For Apollo Tarsios, see *Musée Belge*, 11, 1907, p. 134; Berlin, *Beschreibung*, no. 680; and Apollo Nisyreites, Keil and von Premerstein, *Zweite Reise*, nos. 199 and 202, with discussion on p. 101. The double axe can of course also be a symbol of Zeus, as for instance Zeus Labraundos of Mylasa, but that lies outside the area which we are concerned with.

[25] Madness here is seen as a punishment from the gods, but we can instructively compare the case of Jucundus, in no. 44, where, if we are to take the account at face value, madness was caused by his mother-in-law's machinations. Perhaps we have here further reason to question whether no. 44 is telling us the correct story.

As Helios is closely connected with Apollo (mentioned in the next line in no. 126, assimilated in no. 28), we may be in the presence here, in some cases at least, simply of a balancing concept. As we have balancing busts of Helios and Selene accompanying that of Men on monument 100, so Helios seems simply to balance Men as moon-god on the two-sided relief, no. 2. Such may also be the reason why Zeus Masphalatenos is given the appearance of a Helios-Apollo on the relief of no. 53, and the sun, as well as the moon, may lighten the underworld, as we see from the Plouton Helios and Koure Selene of no. 28, lines 20-21. Here, however, the relation to Men is quite tangential.

In spite of a lack of specific evidence, circumstances point to a fairly close connection between Men and Attis from a fairly early date. To begin with, the iconography is similar, and has led to confusion in the past. Generally, iconographic details used to identify Attis on gems, etc., have been those of a young man with Phrygian cap, the cap usually covered with stars. We have rather arbitrarily, but not unreasonably, I submit, concluded that when the moon-crescent is present, we have Men, but when it is absent, we have Attis. This has caused the reattribution of several monuments most notably the silver plate from the Hildesheim treasure[26] which to my knowledge had always previously been taken to represent Attis.

But there is no question but that exactly similar representations to that on the plate, with starry caps, when occuring on coins, had never been taken to represent anything but Men.[27] Exactly the same head appears on Pessinus, no. 1, and there is no reason, as some

---

[26] *CMRDM*, II, p. 169. The fact that there is a matching plate with Cybele, of course, means nothing for the identification.

[27] Men with starry cap appears on coins of Juliopolis (1, 4, 6, 7, 10, 14), Saittae (4, 5, 6), Attouda (1, 2), Prymnessus (1, 2), Antioch — where certainly there can be not the slightest doubt as to the identification — (1-7, 10, 12-17, 28, 41), Sagalassus (19), Sillyon (4, 28, 30-33, 37, 49), Galatia (2), Ancyra (9), and on gem no. 16.

The close association of Men with Attis and the mother of the gods is also borne out by the reference to him in the Orphic Hymns, T. 10. On the other hand Lucian's passage T. 5 is too eclectic to warrant attaching any particular meaning to it.

numismatists have been inclined to do,[28] to call this head, or any of the other Men-representations on Pessinuntine coins, Attis, just because of what we know of the history of the place. It thus appears that the cult of Men was established in Pessinus from prior to the Roman Imperial period, for coin no. 1 seems to be that early, and Men's connections with the great mother of Pessinus, although not attested in literature, appear to be of long standing. This, of course — without even trying to broach the more complicated question of the great mother herself, whether she is Anatolian, Iranian, Celtic, or a little of each — simply confirms what we have already observed as to Men's association with Cybele in Lydia, although admittedly if he is associated with Attis, he appears now as sexual partner, not as son.[29]

It should come as no surprise, therefore, given the original close relationship between them, that in the late fourth-century inscriptions from Rome (22-27, AD 2-4), confirmed perhaps by the Serdica

[28] E.g., Imhoof-Blumer, *Griechische Münzen*, Munich, 1890, p. 228 (= 452), no. 754, with Pl. 13, no. 11. On the other hand, I would be hesitant to claim for Men such a coin as *ibid.*, no. 748, with Pl. 13, no. 7, which shows jugate busts of a male and a female divinity. I am not convinced that the object in front of the pair of busts is in fact half of a crescent moon. *Men Gallikos*, discussed elsewhere in this monograph, fits into the present context.

[29] In his discussion of our no. A8, *Istanbuler Mitteilungen*, 25, 1975, 357-365, Elmar Schwertheim concludes that Men's mother is Cybele, and emphasizes the similarities between Men and Attis to back up his conclusion. I am quite in agreement with Dr. Schwertheim as to the connections between Men and Attis, and have adduced above even more reasons for the connection than he gives. On the other hand, although Men's mother may be Cybele from an iconographical point of view, I doubt if she bore that name in Lydia, where the preserved inscriptions give other names to the mother goddesses associated with Men.

I disagree with Dr. Schwertheim in that I do not see justification for Cumont's identification (*REA*, 1906, p. 184 ff.) as Men of a riding figure shown in the pediment of a Cybele relief illustrated by Graillot, *Le Culte de Cybèle*, Paris, 1912, p. 359. Pl. I. Likewise, I find it a bit farfetched to see a reference to the cult of Men in a passage of Hippolytus quoted by Schwertheim, although the passage unquestionably shows lunar affinities for Attis: Ἄττι, σὲ καλοῦσι......ἐπουράνιον μηνὸς κέρας Ἕλληνες (*Refutatio*, V, 9; Hippolytus is ostensibly giving the words sung by an actor-devotee of Attis in the theater).

Schwertheim also adduces some interesting passages where Attis, like Men in this inscription, appears as son, rather than lover, of Cybele.

inscription (D 3) and a magical papyrus[30], *Menotyrannus* has simply become an epithet of Attis.

Passing briefly over a joint priesthood with the abstract *Agathos Daimon* (no. 101) and a dedication to Heracles and the people by a priest of Men at Aphrodisias (no. 119), again at least showing the compatibility of the cults, let us come to Men's connection with two widespread and probably more characteristic religious manifestations of Roman Asia Minor: θεὸς ὕψιστος and τὸ θεῖον.

In no. 129, we have a dedication by a priest of Men Ouranios, Quintus Numerius, to *theos hypsistos*. The inscription poses several points of interest, which unfortunately cannot be wholly resolved. In the first place, it is the only place in Men-cult where something is done in accordance with an oracle (κατὰ χρηματισμόν). Although perhaps nothing more may be meant by this than the normal κατ' ἐπιταγήν, the word would seem to me to suggest a more elaborate procedure, in which the worshipper consults the god and receives an answer through some agency or other. We thus are at least in the same general realm as nos. 47 and 50, in which people ask the god for an answer.[31]

Secondly, it is not clear whether Men is here being called *theos hypsistos*, or the priest of Men is simply making a dedication to another god (cf. no. 7). The first possibility, however, is by no means to be ruled out. *Zeus hypsistos* or *theos hypsistos* occurs frequently enough in material from Asia Minor and other parts of the empire. Often it is almost automatically taken as a sign of cryptojudaism,[32] but this certainly is not valid in all, or even the majority of cases.[33] As A. D. Nock *et al.*, say, "Hypsistos was a term in use, vague enough to suit any god treated as the supreme being." In the present case, it is uncertain whether *hypsistos* and Men are one and the same,

---

[30] *Papyri Graecae Magicae*, p. 167, line 2663.
[31] On this word, see L. Robert, *REG*, 64, 1961, p. 244, no. 748. The dice-oracles, nos. 132-136, simply reduce this matter to a banal formalism.
[32] *E.g.*, Barbara Levick in *RE*, Suppl. 14, *s.v. Sibidunda*, col. 675.
[33] See A. D. Nock *et al.*, "The Gild of Zeus Hypsistos," in *Essays on Religion and the Ancient World*, I, no. 22, particularly p. 423 ff.: T. Kraabel. "Hypsistos and the Synagogue at Sardis," *Greek, Roman, and Byzantine Studies*, 10, 1969, p. 81 ff. See also the dedication of ἴχνη above, p. 25.

but in view of the enthusiasm for Men shown at Saittae (no. 83), it cannot, as I said, be ruled out.

The generalized abstraction τὸ θεῖον — familiar enough, say, to readers of Eunapius, as an overall term of pagan monotheism — comes increasingly to be an object of actual dedications and worship in Roman Asia Minor. It is attested in our no. 85 as an associated divinity with Men.[34] This term, as the parallel instances cited by L. Robert show, belongs closely in the same circles with θεὸς ὕψιστος, ὅσιος καὶ δίκαιος, and pagan angels, all subjects discussed elsewhere in this monograph.

Now that we have made a detailed study of the various other divinities who are individually associated with Men, we may be in a better position to elucidate the remarkable syncretistic relief no. 142. Although this unusual piece was published originally almost eight decades ago, and has probably been reillustrated more than any other single monument related to Men-cult, discussion of it remains rather skimpy, probably because of failure to relate it to its context.

On the top we see the bust of Men, Σωτὴρ καὶ Πλουτοδώτης, with long ringlets which give it a feminine appearance. This reminds us of the association which we have remarked on between Men and Selene, and the fact that male sex is not the most important fact about this god. As well as the large crescent below the head, and the two above it, one on a little orb, the head is also decorated with a radiate crown. Here we are in the presence of the Helios-Apollo association which we have noticed before. In the field, to either side of the head, are stars — these recall the iconographic similarity between Men and Attis. On the sides are pairs of torches, which remind us of the association with Demeter at various places in Lydia, of the association with Hecate (herself associated with Demeter as far back as the Homeric Hymn), of the torches carried by Selene, and perhaps more indirectly of the tangential relationship with Pluto and Kore in no. 28 and of the fact that Men, along with the underworld couple, was one of the principal gods of Nysa ad Maeandrum.

[34] See Herrmann and Polatkan, *Das Testament des Epikrates*, p. 54, and L. Robert, *Opera Minora Selecta*, I, 411 (= *Anatolia*, 3, 1958, 112) ff., as well as Kraabel, *art. cit.*, p. 83.

Under the head is a balance, of which the top beam consists of a snake, an appropriate enough symbol for a chthonian divinity. (Cf. the snake on no. 153, which is a combination votive and funerary monument.) Hanging from one end of the balance is a cornucopia, itself also decorated with a crescented snake, reminding us of Men's numismatic association with Tyche, especially at Nysa and Antioch, as well as the wealth-giving function of chthonian divinities, emphasized in the epithet given to Men on this stone. Hanging from the other end are a bow and quiver (?), reminding us of Men's association with Artemis, although, one must admit, it is not elsewhere with Artemis the huntress. Directly under the snake-balance and supporting it on its two horns, is a bucranium, one of the commonest symbols of Men, although nowhere else, admittedly, with this Cyclopean appearance.

Wedged in between the snake and the bucranium are two round objects: if taken to be pomegranates, they too could be underworld symbolism. Between them is a small object, perhaps intended for a rudder (but if so, quite different from the standard ancient rudder-representation), and thus associated with Tyche. On one side of the bull's head, we see a syrinx, reminding us of Pan, a god with whom Men is associated a couple of times in the Attic material, whereas on the other side there is apparently a pruning-hook — this latter must remain preliminarily unexplained, unless one cares to speculate about Dionysus, the god of viticulture.[35]

Springing out from either side of the nose of the bucranium are two more rudders, normally shaped this time, again symbolic of Men's direction of affairs and his association with Tyche. Towards the bottom of the relief, which is even more cluttered than the top, the parallelisms between this piece and other associations of Men start to break down. The vertical axis, below the bull's head, consists, top to bottom, of a large dish of fruits and leaves, propped on the head and hands of a nude figure, whose torso emerges from

[35] Cf. the parallelisms between the objects on this relief and the crossed rudder and cornucopia or crossed torch and cornucopia on the reverses of Sardis coins 1 and 2. I generally leave reverses of coins out of consideration in these discussions, as they by no means necessarily have any connection with the obverses, but occasionally one runs into cases where they contribute to the discussion.

behind the next figure down. The dish obviously symbolizes Men as giver of wealth. The figure from behind which the dish-carrier emerges is a goat, not an animal normally associated with Men,[36] in spite of the crescent plastered on its side. Finally, at the bottom, we see the pine-cone, one of the most widespread Men-symbols of all.

The area to the left of the central axis is occupied with a variety of things — a winged caduceus, probably symbolic of Men's connection with Hermes, which we have already had occasion to mention; the caps of the Dioscuri (not elsewhere known to have been associated with Men unless one counts the reverse of Timbrias coin 1), and a pair of tongs (surgical equipment? attributes of Hephaistos?).

In addition, there are other fruits of the field, including what may be another pomegranate; another bucranium; a sheep;[37] and a long-legged waterbird.

On the right of the main axis, we find a winged mirror (perhaps inspired by the disk worn on the head of Isis); a wheel of Nemesis or Fortune; a crowlike bird, unattested elsewhere in the cult of Men; a squid, likewise unattested and of unclear meaning; a lion whose tail turns into a snake, likewise anomalous and unparalleled; and in the extreme right bottom corner, an indistinct object which I would not venture to identify.

This survey, therefore, of the associations of Men with other gods has revealed a rich and varied set of associations with other divinities both male and female, even neuter. The association with a mother-goddess, mentioned at the outset as something almost taken for granted about "Anatolian" divinities, has turned out to be only one, albeit an important one, among many associations, and that — leaving aside the Men-Attis syncretism —, where it is clearly expressed, sees Men as the son, rather than the consort, of the mother-goddess.

I have so far left out of consideration the gods associated with Attis Menotyrannus in the inscriptions which mention him, all from

[36] Cf., however, the goat's heads which adorn no. 30, or the goat which appears as reverse type of Antioch coin no. 22.

[37] Again, not an animal normally associated with Men, but cf. nos. 1, 2, 3, and 85.

fourth-century Rome. But it should come as no surprise to us that they conform pretty closely to those gods whom we have already seen to be associated with Men alone.

To begin with, the dedications are invariably made to the Great Idaean Mother and Attis Menotyrannus, probably conceived of as her consort here. In no. 23 Hermes (N.B., not Mercury) is joined as the god of magic, one might suppose; we have already mentioned the relation of Hermes to Men. The devotees are themselves priests and functionaries of other cults in most cases — Hecate (nos. 24, 27, AD 3[38]); Isis (AD 4); Liber (= Dionysus, nos. 24-27); Sol (= Helios, no. 25); Proserpina (= Kore, no. AD 2). Only Mithras (nos. 24, 26, 27, and AD 3), in whose cult most of the male dedicants hold some office, is a newcomer.

---

[38] Hecate must also be somehow involved in the *Triodeia signa* of AD 3. I have left aside as probably irrelevant the verse ending to this inscription.

CHAPTER SEVEN

THE ICONOGRAPHY OF MEN

Men is nearly always shown standing or riding, rarely seated. The instances in which he is shown seated can be numbered on the fingers of one hand: the coin Gangra 1, the statuette 140, and the baby-Men, no. 64.

Riding is somewhat more common. Whatever one may speculate its reason to be, great distances to cover, or the like, it is a well-known fact that divinities in Asia Minor and the Danube area are frequently shown on horseback. Certainly, however, one is not justified in concluding from that that there is any identity among these gods.[1]

Men is shown riding in relief on monuments 78, 87, 91 (if indeed Men is intended), 94, 104, 107, 112, 122-125, 128, and D 9. Of these, almost all whose provenience can be pinpointed come from interior Asia Minor, Phrygia or Pisidia, the only significant exception being 78, from Sardis. Free-standing representations of Men riding are provided by no. 139 (terracotta), no. 159 (stone), and the newly discovered bronze statuette A 11, on which, however, a new horse has been substituted for the original.

Coin representations, too, show Men riding, and there seem to have been certain cities with a particular liking for the type.[2] Now

[1] The idea of the one rider-god was put to rest by L. Robert's remarks on Kaskabos, *Hellenica*, 3, p. 59: "Le fait que ces dieux sont representés à cheval ne suffit certes pas à établir entre eux une unité fondamentale. N'en est-il pas un peu pour les dieux comme pour les hommes? Le fait d'être à cheval n'établit pas une ressamblance radicale entre deux hommes."

[2] The complete list is:
Juliopolis 2, 3, 5, 8.
Alia 4, 5, 6, 7 (the last three, at least, with the double axe, a local peculiarity).
Apameia 1.
Eriza 1.
Hadrianopolis 3.
Hydrela 2, 3, 4, 5.
Julia 1, 2.
Ariassus 1.

it becomes apparent from the listing given in the footnote that the riding type is entirely absent from the Lydian, Carian, and more coastward areas, even such major cult centers as Nysa seems to have been. Alia ties the riding type to a local iconographical variant, and some other places use it exclusively or heavily out of a rather limited overall number of Men-types which they strike — Apameia, Eriza, Hadrianopolis, Hydrela, Julia, Ariassus, Olbasa. On the other hand, Pisidian places such as Baris, Sagalassus, and Seleuceia, which have fairly extensive Men-coinages, use the riding type rather sparingly. Nor can it pass without notice that the great cult-center at Antioch in Pisidia seems not to use the riding type at all.

Oddly enough, two of the places at which the riding type is most popular lie at the north and south fringes of the hinterland area — Juliopolis of Bithynia, where the riding type accounts for four of the seventeen types I have recorded, and Sillyon of Pamphylia, where it accounts for twenty-one out of fifty-four. We must also remark that Sillyon is second only to Antioch in total variety of Men-types, and as we know from coins 53 and 54 was the ἄσυλον of Men. The cult there, as at Nysa, must have been very important, and only imperfect exploration seems to be at fault for the fact that our information is not filled out with epigraphical records.

At Laodiceia ad Libanum, in Syria, a location quite remote from normal centers of Men-cult, there is a special variant on this iconographical type. Perhaps one should speculate on a local Semitic god, who because of iconographical or — to us unknown — mythological similarity, was assimilated to the better-known Men of Anatolia. This type, exclusive on the Men-coinage of the city, shows Men standing, holding a horse by the bridle. In two cases (nos. 3 and 4) he is also holding a torch, an attribute frequently enough connected with him, and reminiscent of his association with Demeter and of his chthonian connections. There can be no doubt but that to the worshippers of this god and to the users of these coins, Men was the

Baris 2, 4.
Olbasa 1, 2, 3, 4 (of which 3 shows him with a shield, likewise a local peculiarity).
Sagalassus 6, 10, 26.
Seleuceia 5, 7, 12, 13.
Sillyon 1, 2, 5, 6, 9, 15, 19, 20, 22, 24, 25, 35, 36, 43, 47, 50, 51, 53.

name of the divinity illustrated. It may be significant, however, that at this outpost of Men-cult, people felt compelled to label him for purposes of identifiability. This is paralleled only by the *Mensis* of the colonial coins of Antioch in Pisidia, where apparently there was a need felt to label the god by or for the Latin-speaking inhabitants of the city. Elsewhere that Men is labeled, it is with a by-name, so that this particular Men can be distinguished from others.[3]

Now Men riding is usually, as one would expect, shown riding a horse. But there are occasions where he is shown riding something else. This occurs among the already anomalous and early Attic material, with its standard type of small worshippers, an offering table, and a large Men on a mount of some kind. In nos. 1, 2, and 3, we see him riding a ram. This is not an animal normally elsewhere occurring with Men, the only at all close parallels being the ram's heads of no. 85.

On no. 14, Men is apparently riding, or at least sitting sidesaddle on a panther, but there is no real certainty as to the identity of the animal. (I have seen a rather poor photograph of this terracotta, but not the object itself.) To the best of my knowledge, there is no parallel for the connection of Men with the panther. The only other felines that occur in Men-iconography are lions, an almost banal symbol of power.[4]

On one Attic relief (no. 10) Men is shown riding a chicken. Although this is the only instance in which he has so unusual a mount (chicken-riders are paralleled on lamps, a fact which led C. Grandjouan to conclude that all chicken-riders were Men), there can be no denying that the chicken has an important role to play in Men-cult in general. On other Attic reliefs (nos. 1-4) we see several

---

[3] Nysa 4 and 5, perhaps 6, have only Καμαρείτης, the by-name, without Μήν. Saittae 4, 5, and 6, have only 'Αξιοττηνός, the by-name, without Μήν; Sardis 1-4 have Μὴν 'Ασκαηνός perhaps a necessary clarification in an area where other Mens, such as *Axiottenos* and *Tiamou*, are commoner; finally Attouda 1 shows us Μὴν Κάρου. Κάρου by itself would have been grammatically unable to stand alone.

[4] Lions flank Men on monuments nos. 50, and 65, as well as on the coins of Gordus-Julia (2, 5-8), Nysa (?) 6, and on the temple-type of Prostanna. It may be possible to take them as a sign of Men's affinity to Cybele and other mother goddesses.

chickens located under or near the offering table, and in no. 6, Men is clutching a chicken to his chest.

But the use of chickens is by no means restricted to the Attic material. The baby-Men of no. 64 is holding a rooster on his knee, and there are preserved traces of a chicken's feet on the base of no. 175, apparently a miniature of the cult-statue from Antioch in Pisidia. Prostanna, too, has chickens beside Men's head on the temple-type coins which it issues. It is particularly the Antiochene type and its imitations which proliferate the number of chickens in Men-iconography. Not only is the chicken present on all coins of Antioch from Antoninus Pius onwards, at least those coins which conform to the normal type, but the chicken also appears on some of the undated Roman-period small denominations (nos. 18, 19). The chicken is also present on some of the imitations of the Antiochene type elsewhere (Parlais 1, Ancyra 7), as well as on the gem G 6. This connection of the chicken with Men would also seem to have found reflection, albeit confusedly, in the passage of Iamblichus cited among the testimonia, T. 8, as well as in that from Diogenes Laertius, T. 7.

This discussion of Men's various mounts has drifted over into a more general consideration of animals that are iconographically associated with him. Of these, unquestionably the most important is the bull, often by shorthand reduced to a bucranium. Whatever the origin of this connection may be — certainly there seems to be a strong presence of bulls in Iranian moon-lore, and the Iranian element seems prominent in Men — and whatever use of the bull's head may have been dictated by the convenient fact that the horns can easily be made to resemble a crescent, two ways of understanding the bull by actual Roman-period worshippers stand out from the material which we have collected.

The first is that the bull is the sacrificial animal *par excellence*. This is clear from such monuments as nos. 177 and 288, perhaps AD 1, all from Antioch, where a bull is tied to an altar as an intended offering. In the text of no. 50 (Lydia) we have it explicitly stated that a bull was promised as an offering, but that the stele was accepted as a substitute.

Secondly, it is hard to avoid the impression that Men is sometimes seen as overcoming or subduing a bull. Although we have no explicit mythology in written form to back up such an interpretation, it is difficult to reach any other *prima facie* conclusion from the defeated-looking bulls on whose heads Men places one foot in the reliefs of nos. 54 and 102. On the other hand, on coins Sagalassus 4 and Timbrias 2, 3, 4 (I incline to this interpretation now, rather than seeing an altar there), a whole bull saunters out from behind Men without looking particularly dejected.

All in all, however, the number of instances where a bucranium occurs, frequently with Men's foot on it — apparently a carry-over from the subduing type —, is very great. The bucranium was, for instance, a standard feature on the Antiochene type, and in these representations Men places his foot squarely on it, as we see from monument no. 175, from the standard Antiochene Men-type from Antoninus Pius onward and from imitations of the Antiochene type elsewhere.[5] Nor is it likely to be purely coincidental that the humped bull is the commonest reverse on pre-Roman Men-coins of Antioch (nos. 1-13), and continues to be used on the small change of Roman times (nos. 20-21).[6]

Certainly the massive amount of material containing these features should convince us that the bull or bucranium is one of Men's most important symbols. Furthermore, the number of instances in which he places his foot or his staff on the bucranium, or has his horse do so, can probably be viewed as shorthand for the subjugation motif, and leads us to suspect that if only the mythology

[5] Siblia 4 and 5, unless this is to be taken as a mule's head; Lysinia 1; Parlais 1 (in general all the Men-coins of Parlais include a bucranium, even if no other of the Antiochene attributes); Ancyra 7, 10, 13, and 15; and gem no. 6.

[6] Other bucrania occur on monuments nos. 98, 110, 123 (under the foot of Men's horse); 137 (under Men's foot), and the motif of a bucranium with a foot placed on it caused the inclusion of D 6. On coins, we find bucrania on Magnesia 9; Nysa 25, 28, 31-33, and 38; Cidrama 1 (under Men's foot); Accilaeum 1 (likewise); Colossae 2 (under end of Men's staff); Hierapolis 1-8 (under Men's foot); Julia 4 (where Men with bucranium is shown in a temple and may thus represent an actual cult-image); Laodiceia 1 (under Men's foot); Baris 1, 3, 5, 7 (likewise); Colbasa 1 and 2 (likewise); Palaeopolis 3 and 4 (under end of Men's staff); Pappa-Tiberia 1 (under Men's foot); Sibidunda 1 (likewise); Attaleia 1 (likewise); Sillyon 3, 10-13, 16, 26, 29, and 34 (likewise); Ancyra 14 (likewise); and G 2 (likewise).

were known, the subduing of the bull would play an important role in it.

We have drifted aside from the main thread of our argument — whether Men is shown sitting, riding, or standing — to discuss animals associated with Men, and lastly the prominence of the bull or bucranium in Men's iconography. Let us now return to the main concern of our argument.

Men is shown standing in the vast majority of cases. He is rarely empty-handed. His left hand usually holds a staff or scepter of some sort, sometimes, as in nos. 50 and 102, with an exceptionally broad point. His right hand most commonly holds a patera, out of which he pours a libation, or it can hold a pine-cone. On the coins, because of small scale, careless engraving, or poor preservation (or all three), it is often almost impossible to distinguish the object carried, so I will forbear trying to give a complete list.[7]

The monuments, however, allow us to determine a little better what Men is holding. On nos. 1, 10, and 140, it is clear that Men is holding a patera for libations. This is a type which, as is well known, goes far back in Ancient Greek iconography, particularly numismatic.[8] Still, I do not know whether it has ever been satisfactorily explained why a *god* should be pouring libations.[9]

Coins which show an altar near Men's feet and under his outstretched hand can fairly safely be assumed to show Men pouring a libation, whether the object in the hand is identifiable or not. Such is the case with Juliopolis 9, 12, and 13, Magnesia 6 and 8, Trapezopolis 1 and 5, Cibyra 2, 4, and 5, Conana 4, Ancyra 6, 11, and 12, and Pessinus 3. Finally we see on Sillyon 18 Men before what is probably a very large altar, but possibly also a fountain-house or a stele.[10]

The second commonly-carried attribute is the pine-cone. Again,

---

[7] Suffice it to refer the reader to such a coin as Cibyra 3 to show the difficulty of identifying the object held even on a relatively well-preserved coin.

[8] See, for instance, the fifth-century B.C. coins of Selinus illustrated by Kenneth Jenkins, *Coins of Greek Sicily*, London, 1966, Plate 5.

[9] Lommel, *art. cit.*, assumes that a god is shown sacrificing to set a model for others.

[10] Cf. also G 8, G 12, and G 15, discussed below under the Galatian type.

because of the difficulty of determining what is intended on coins, I spare the reader a complete listing of numismatic examples. On the monuments, however, the pine-cone can be discerned with varying degrees of certainty on nos. 50, 54, 64-66, 69, 90, 102, 104, 112, 123, 127, 137, 138, 159, A8 and A11. In addition, the presence of the pine-cone caused the inclusion of no. D1. The pine-cone is a fairly obvious symbol of vegetative regeneration and new life, and is used not only by Men-cult, but is one of the most familiar symbols of Sabazius-cult. In Men-cult, however, it seems restricted to Asia Minor.[11]

Occasionally, Men can be found holding other attributes. It is fairly certain that a few, at least, of the monuments show Men holding a bunch of grapes, although iconographically it is difficult enough to tell a bunch of grapes from a patera with a libation pouring out of it. At all events, grapes are assuredly shown on the secondary relief fields of monuments 107 and 108, possibly on that of 128, and seem fairly definitely to be held by Men on Apollonia coin 2. Grapes may be seen as a crop particularly under Men's patronage, or could point to his association with Dionysus.

Some of the special aberrant representations of Men have already been treated in the preceding chapter, in connection with the associations and syncretisms of Men with other gods. There are some, however, which do not fit this category, and must be mentioned separately here.

We have already had occasion to mention that Antioch in Pisidia had a cult-statue of distinct type, which is illustrated on the coins of that city, and the fame of which spread abroad even as far as Ancyra and influenced coin types elsewhere.

Certain other places, too, seem to have had their own cult-statue which gives rise to particular local iconographic types on their coins. Most notable is (Claudio)seleuceia. The Men-coins of this city, except 5, 7, 12, and 13, which show him riding, show him in a peculiar pose in which he holds a staff in his right hand, but nothing in his left. Rather he places his left hand on his hip, and bends his left knee up noticeably in order to place his left foot on a bucranium.

---

[11] See the discussion of the symbolism of the pine-cone in Cumont's chapter "La Lune Séjour des Morts" in his *Symbolisme Funéraire*.

As I said, the type is uniform for all standing Mens at Seleuceia, but is not found elsewhere. The reasonable inference is that we have here the reflection of a local cult-statue.

The Koinon of the Galatians, likewise, seems to have had a peculiar type, also inspired by a local cult-statue. This type (Galatia 3-6) shows Men standing with patera in outstretched right hand, his left hand down at his side, sometimes seeming to be holding a pine-cone, sometimes seeming to be empty. So far as I can determine, this same type is also represented in the small figure in the temple shown on Galatia no. 7, and this would confirm the idea that we are dealing here with a cult-image. This type spread to Ancyra (coin 2) and Pessinus (coin 4), both cities within Galatia, and with the addition of an altar and a cock, to G 8, G 12, and G 15. This is also the reason for the attribution usually given to the Galba-coin which we have classed as "Uncertain, perhaps Ancyra."[12]

The city of Ancyra itself, although the capital of the Galatians, and presumably the religious center of the *koinon*, does not in general adhere to the *koinon*'s model in coinage. More popular is the punning type, in which Men holds an anchor (Ancyra 3 and 5) as a symbol of the city. This type, incidentally, shows that Men was considered pretty much as divinity *poliouchos* at Ancyra. In Ancyra also we have the greatest concentration of representations of Men in strikingly military costume (nos. 6, 11, and 12). This phenomenon is not unparalleled. Olbasa 3 shows us a riding Men carrying a large shield, and monument no. 112 also has a distinctly military look to it. On monument 99, a militarily dressed Men carries a palm-branch, apparently a symbol of a victory of some kind, and of course there is the victory which Men carries on the Antiochene type and its derivatives. Likewise coherent with this circle of iconography is the laurel wreath with which his Phrygian cap is often adorned.[13] All

[12] *CMRDM*, II, p. 160.
[13] Pharnaceia 1; Alia 1 (?); Antioch 8, 10, 12-17 (all pre-Roman); Sagalassus 1, 5, 19, and G 3. The shields, if that is what they are, on the antae of the Prostanna temple, are to be compared with the Olbasa coin.

Sabine Schultz, *Staatliche Museen zu Berlin, Forschungen und Berichte*, 16, *Archäologische Beiträge*, Berlin-Ost, 1975, p. 235 tentatively identifies the object which Men holds in his left hand on Magnesia 1, etc., as a shield seen from the side. If so, we have additional evidence of Men as a military god. She also (p. 234 with Pl. 30, 17) publishes a coin of Magnesia which shows

in all wreaths are a common enough feature of Men-cult, particularly at Antioch, a phenomenon which we have already had occasion to comment upon.[14]

Although Men is distinctly not a soldier's god (there are only two monuments from the *limes*, both from Dacia), it does not require much imagination to see that he was sometimes conceived of as a soldier in the metaphorical sense, winning the palm or wreath of victory over evil or perhaps (no. 99) over death itself.

Finally let me mention the unique reverse of Nysa 29, which shows Men recumbent as a river god. This coin, so unexpected that both Drexler and Regling dismiss it from consideration, still assumes a greater comprehensibility if placed in context, something which is possible only after an attempt to gather all the evidence, as I have tried to do.

Although there are no parallels for Men as a river-god, there is evidence of his strong connection with rivers elsewhere in the Lydian area. Not only does the reverse of Sardis 3 pair Men with the river-god Hermus (we have already seen on p. 96 how the reverses of Sardis 1 and 2 are likewise not irrelevant for an interpretation of Men-cult), but Saittae 4 and 5 have reverses that pair Men with the Hermos and Hyllos, the two rivers near which the city lay, and Saittae 3, 17, and 18 go out of their way to show Men standing between the two recumbent rivers.

Putting all this together, and remembering Men's function of rain-god in the Attic inscription no. 5, it appears that Men has a consistent connection with rivers, at least in Lydia. Rivers, of course, with all their potential beneficial qualities as givers of agricultural wealth, but also all their potential destructiveness, fit the general picture which we have already acquired of this god.

All in all, then, the effort which we have made in collecting all this evidence for the cult of Men and examining the iconography as a whole, rather than in segments, has paid off in a wider understand-

---

a Nike with the moon crescent at her shoulders, a sort of reverse example of the association which we have been discussing.

[14] Nos. 70 and 71 (Lydian funerary reliefs); 249, 250, 253, 261, 267, 271, 282, 283, 287, 291 and 293 (Antioch); 110 (N. Phrygia).

ing of the cult and in filling some of the gaps left by the absence of any written mythology. The conclusions which can be reached about Men subduing the bull, Men as a victorious soldier (at least metaphorically), and Men as a river-god, would seem to merit particular consideration.

CHAPTER EIGHT

THE WORSHIPPERS OF MEN; MISCELLANEOUS

The subject of the worshippers of Men, their social standing, is a topic which we have had occasion to touch on already, particularly in reference to the Attic material, but I would like to try to draw the threads of it together here.

As far as the Attic material is concerned, it has generally been held that the Men-cult was restricted to slaves. This conclusion is largely based on the Sounion inscriptions, nos. 11-13, and assumes that Xanthus, himself apparently a slave as he gives his owner's name, founded the cult exclusively for the benefit of his fellow slaves. These slaves, presumably, were those who worked in the silver mines at Laurion, suitable enough worshippers for a god with subterranean connections.[1]

This interpretation of the Sounion inscriptions, reasonable enough in itself, has led to the generalization that in Attica at least Men-cult was "ein ausgesprochener Sklavenkultus."[2] Only F. Bömer has pointed out that the handbook-statement does not necessarily hold water,[3] at least as far as the earlier, Hellenistic material is concerned. According to him, and in this view I concur, all the Hellenistic dedications seem to have been made by metics. The only one which with any probability, but without certainty, may be ascribed to a slave, and that on the basis of name alone, is no. 10.

On Delos, we really know nothing about the dedicants. Perdrizet's association of the name Τάοσα with a name recorded in a sixth-century A.D. Christian inscription is little enough to go on.[4] Only in nos. 20 and 21 do we have Roman soldiers, Gaius Petronius Iustus and Aur. Marcianus, making dedications to Men, both in Dacia. It would seem reasonable to suppose that they became

[1] The fullest statement of this theory is to be found in S. Lauffer, *Akad. der Wissenschaften und der Literatur, Mainz, Geistes- und Sozialwissenschaftliche Klasse, Abhandlungen*, 1956, 11, p. 179 (= 943) ff.
[2] M. P. Nilsson, *Geschichte der griechischen Religion*, II, p. 630.
[3] *Mainz Akad., Abhandlungen*, 1961, 4, p. 195 (= 437) ff.
[4] *BCH*, 20, 1896, p. 75, note 2.

acquainted with the cult in the course of previous military service in Asia Minor.

On Rhodes, as we have already had occasion to mention, Men is worshipped by an association which calls itself Μηνιασταί (nos. 16 and 17), and it is likely that the honorand of no. 17 had migrated to Rhodes from the great cult-center of Antioch in Pisidia. The same pattern of group-worship is found in a number of inscriptions, presumably of later date, from Asia Minor. Specifically, we have the two φράτραι of nos. 87 and 127, the ἱερὸς δοῦμος or ἱερὰ συμβίωσις of nos. 53 and 54, or specific cultic organizations such as the συμβολαφόροι of no. 57 or the καταλουστικοί of nos. 34 and A3. Also to be mentioned in this connection are the mysterious Menagyrtai of about 300 B.C., who appear to have been mendicant priests of Men in Attica.[5] A reflection of this group worship is probably to be found in the ἔρανος for which provision is made in no. 13, line 21.

As far as the mass of the Lydian material is concerned, it would seem reasonable to me to see in the bulk of the dedicants free peasantry. As we have already pointed out, the idea of a theocracy in this area seems far-fetched. Certainly slaves are at pains to point out their servile status, either explicitly or by mentioning their masters' names: no. 33 δοῦλος; no. 72, δοῦλος πραγματευτής; no. 80, οἰκονόμος, accompanied by a name in the genitive. Arguments from silence are dangerous, but it seems likely that other dedicants would likewise have drawn attention to their servile status had they been slaves.[6]

Professions are not mentioned extensively in the Lydian material. Apart from the πραγματευτής and the οἰκονόμος we have the τοπίαρις of no. 85. According to J. and L. Robert's convincing interpretation,[7] this is a Greek spelling of the Latin *topiarius*, "landscape gardener."

---

[5] I have already said all that I think I can say about them on the basis of present evidence, *Berytus*, 17, 1967-8, p. 90, Appendix I.

[6] Bömer, *op. cit.*, p. 205 (= 447) states, "Unter den angehörigen dieser (sc. lydischen) Kulte sind keine Sklaven erkennbar." Certainly, if it provides any parallel, the priest of Artemis Anaeitis honored by a *doumos*, Herrmann, *Ergebnisse*, no. 25, is not only free, but a Roman citizen, in the year 223/4, after the Constitutio Antoniniana, as is the priest of Isis and Sarapis who worships Men in no. 7.

[7] *REG*, 83, 1970, Bulletin Epigraphique, no. 522.

Since he does not call himself δοῦλος, nor does he mention a master, it may be supposed that he is a free man.

Asklepias in no. 90[8] describes herself as κώμης Κερυζέων πα(ι)-δίσχη, which is probably to be interpreted as slave-girl, perhaps even prostitute.[9] The genitive of the place-name leaves uncertain, to my mind, whether she was simply *from* that place, or actually a public slave *of* that place (it is hard to see a κώμη, however, having enough governmental structure to support public slaves). Perhaps she was a temple-slave, but in that case you would expect the situation to have been expressed more explicitly.[10]

At Antioch in Pisidia, we have the second major source of knowledge of people's professions and social standing among Men-worshippers in Asia Minor. A variety of professions are indicated. In no. 203, P. Viteilius, who has a Latin name, describes himself as τέκτων. In no. 217, Alexandros calls himself ζωγράφος. Protion, the dedicant of 163 and 255 describes himself with the phrase τὸν Μοῦσαι θρέψαντο and must therefore have been a man of some education, also.[11] Among the free-standing dedications from Antioch, the unnamed dedicant of 283 calls himself κοπτοπώλης, or "confectioner."[12] T. Claudius Pasinianus Neos of no. 290 describes himself as *summa rudis*, i.e., an ex-gladiator fencing master, a person of no small prominence in the community.[13] Finally, the freedman dedicant of no. 160, Ti. Claudius Epinicus, had apparently risen so high at Rome that he could call himself *procurator et praegustator et a secretis Augusti*, and then had returned home to be a *sevir Augustalis* in his native town.[14]

[8] See my article "Two notes on Lydian Topography," *Anatolian Studies*, 25, 1975, p. 110, for arguments that this place is likely to be in the Kula-area.
[9] See *LSJ*, s.v.
[10] For known *hierodouloi* of the area, see Herrmann, *Ergebnisse*, no. 45 and note 200.
[11] See Barbara Levick, *Roman Colonies in Southern Asia Minor*, Oxford, 1967, p. 125.
[12] See B. Levick and A. M. Davies, *Classical Review*, 1971, pp. 162-166, for speculation on the possible sacral character of the confections made and their connection with the offering cakes shown on the Attic reliefs.
[13] See L. Robert, *Les Gladiateurs dans l'Orient Grec*, Limoges, 1940, p. 263.
[14] Levick remarks, *Roman Colonies*, p. 88, that this man "may have been wealthy, but belonged by birth to the lower classes."

If the Antonine-period statue inscribed Κορνηλία Ἀντωνία (J. Inan and

But this gets us out of the matter of profession and into that of the general social standing of the votaries of Men at Antioch in Pisidia. Even the most cursory glance will show that the dedicants have a hodge-podge of names — Roman names, often enough written in Greek, belonging either to members of old Roman families or to freedmen; Greek names; and some odd ones that may be native.[15] Extreme caution must be exercised, however, in trying to read these names, particularly those on the sanctuary wall, as the type of stone they are cut into and the state of preservation makes certainty in some cases virtually impossible.[16]

Barbara Levick has done the scholarly world a great favor with her analysis of the Roman names of Antioch in Pisidia. The Ἥουιος of no. 191 she equates with Evius, probably a name of Etruscan origin.[17] Netrius (no. 234) and Vacarnius (no. 235) are also apparently Latin names, but Levick is unable to provide any parallels. As to Οὐενουάος (no. 240), Levick is unable to decide whether it is a Latin or a native name. No. 279 provides a name which Miss Levick[18] interprets as Visennius, and again sees an Etruscan origin.[19]

More important than these names, however, are such names as that of C. Anicius Q. f. Ser. Caesianus (A 10), who is a member of the Anicii, a leading family in the Roman colony.[20] Another ap-

E. Rosenbaum, *Roman and Early Byzantine Portrait Sculpture in Asia Minor*, London, 1966, p. 206, no. 287, from Yalvaç, now in Istanbul) is of the same person as the dedicant of our 256, then we are dealing here also with a person of wealth and importance.

[15] E.g. Αὔγμης (no. 192), or Λόλου (no. 186). The latter is listed by L. Zgusta in his *Kleinasiatische Personennamen*, Prague, 1966, but he knows no parallels.

[16] See no. 193 as an example of the different readings that can be proposed for the same inscription. If Ramsay is correct, then we have here another example of communal worship of Men.

[17] *Roman Colonies*, p. 65; this name, which also occurs several other times in this area, has also, but with less probability, been considered native. In the bad light of the Konya museum I read Ἡούλειος = Julius.

[18] *Op. cit.*, p. 64.

[19] By the time of her article in *Anatolian Studies*, 20, 1970, however, Miss Levick had hesitantly opted for *Usellius* instead. My reading in the Konya museum was closer to her first interpretation.

[20] Levick, *op. cit.*, p. 117. If Ramsay's dating is right, this is also an early inscription. We have remarked elsewhere on the fact that the priests of Men elsewhere in central Asia Minor seem to be important and wealthy people of their communities.

parently aristocratic name is Calpurnius (nos. 226 and 280, although in the latter case the persons are definitely freedmen). The fact that a duovir of the colony makes the donation for the gymnastic contest at the moon-festival, which we consider to be connected with Men (no. 178), speaks as eloquently as anything can for the respectability of the cult in high Roman circles.[21]

After this survey of what is known about the worshippers, let me conclude with some observations about the origin of the cult, a topic already suggested by the mention of Roman favor made above. This, of course, is a topic that immediately presents itself to the student of religion, and one to which I have already addressed myself elsewhere.[22] Since it is not, however, necessarily an easy question to answer, it would not be inappropriate to recapitulate here some of my previously presented ideas.

My personal view is that there is no real evidence for seeing Men as an indigenous Anatolian divinity. The large temple estates described by Strabo as existing at Antioch in Pisidia prior to the planting of a Roman colony there could easily have grown up in a matter of a few hundred years — even since the foundation of the Seleucid colony there. The same applies to the temple estates in Pontus.[23] Further, none of the Attic material need antedate the opening up of the East by Alexander.

The principal element in the cult seems to be Persian, as evidenced by the association with Anahita, the iconographic similarity to the Persian moon-spirit Mao, the use of Men as oath-god by the Pontic kings, who claimed Iranian descent, and the prominence of the bull in the cult's iconography. Not least important, it was probably the Persian Mao who determined the name Μήν or Μείς for the god we have been studying.

[21] A fact which I have underlined both in my article "The Italian Connection," *Numen*, 22, 1975, pp. 235-239, and in my article for *Aufstieg und Niedergang der römischen Welt*.

[22] Particularly in *Berytus*, 17, 1967-8, pp. 81-106 and in my article for *Aufstieg und Niedergang der römischen Welt*.

[23] Mr. H. Bartlett Wells of Washington, D.C., brings to my attention a coin of Anemurium, *Sylloge Nummorum Graecorum*, Sammlung von Aulock, 5517, of the second century A.D., which is overstruck AMEPIA. This interesting piece would seem to attest the continued mercantile importance of the sanctuary of Men Pharnakou at a much later date than Strabo.

Although the Persian component may be important in the *actual history* of the cult, this is not to say that the worshippers necessarily understood the cult in this light. It is clear that Men-cult was readily acclimatized in Asia Minor, and we have already seen that Men establishes affinities with various gods, not least among them Attis (whom we shall assume, at least for present purposes, to be indigenous Anatolian).

I have elsewhere devoted a full article[24] to showing that Men could at least be supposed to have multifarious connections with Italy, a fact which the Romans seized upon for their own propagandistic purposes in order to secure the allegiance of their Anatolian subjects.

We are thus in the presence of a highly complex cult, with many facets, some of which are still far from being completely understood. None of them should be emphasized to the neglect of others, and it is hoped that the present study has helped rectify some of the imbalance in previous scholarship. I have no delusions about having said everything that can be said, or even everything that ought to be said, about this cult or about the social and religious context within which it flourished. I hope, however, to have given a somewhat more rounded and complete picture than has been available hitherto, and to have laid the groundwork for future scholarship.

[24] *Numen*, 22, 1975, pp. 235-239.

TESTIMONIA ANTIQUA

T. 1. Strabo, XII, iii, 31 (ed. H. L. Jones, Loeb Classical Library 1928, 1961[4]):

Ταύτην δὴ τὴν χώραν ἔχει πᾶσαν ἡ Πυθοδωρίς, προσεχῆ οὖσαν τῇ βαρβάρῳ τῇ ὑπ' αὐτῆς κατεχομένῃ, καὶ τὴν Ζηλῖτιν καὶ Μεγαλοπολῖτιν. τὰ δὲ Κάβειρα, Πομπηίου σκευάσαντος εἰς πόλιν καὶ καλέσαντος Διόσπολιν, ἐκείνη προσκατεσκεύασε καὶ Σεβαστὴν μετωνόμασε, βασιλείῳ τε τῇ πόλει χρῆται. ἔχει δὲ καὶ τὸ ἱερὸν Μηνὸς Φαρνάκου καλούμενον, τὴν Ἀμερίαν κωμόπολιν πολλοὺς ἱεροδούλους ἔχουσαν καὶ χώραν ἱεράν, ἣν ὁ ἱερώμενος ἀεὶ καρποῦται. ἐτίμησαν δ' οἱ βασιλεῖς τὸ ἱερὸν τοῦτο οὕτως εἰς ὑπερβολήν, ὥστε τὸν βασιλικὸν καλούμενον ὅρκον τοῦτον ἀπέφηναν Τύχην βασιλέως καὶ Μῆνα Φαρνάκου. ἔστι δὲ καὶ τοῦτο τῆς Σελήνης τὸ ἱερόν, καθάπερ τὸ ἐν Ἀλβανοῖς καὶ τὰ ἐν Φρυγίᾳ, τό τε τοῦ Μηνὸς ἐν τῷ ὁμωνύμῳ τόπῳ καὶ τὸ τοῦ Ἀσκαίου τὸ πρὸς Ἀντιοχείᾳ τῇ πρὸς Πισιδίᾳ καὶ τὸ ἐν τῇ χώρᾳ τῶν Ἀντιοχέων.

T. 2. Strabo, XII, viii, 14 (The Ἀρκαίου of the MSS is to be emended into Ἀσκαίου):

Ἡ μὲν οὖν Παρώρεια ὀρεινήν τινα ἔχει ῥάχιν ἀπὸ τῆς ἀνατολῆς ἐκτεινομένην ἐπὶ δύσιν. ταύτῃ δ' ἑκατέρωθεν ὑποπέπτωκέ τι πεδίον μέγα καὶ πόλεις πλησίον αὐτῆς, πρὸς ἄρκτον μὲν Φιλομήλιον, ἐκ θατέρου δὲ μέρους Ἀντιόχεια ἡ πρὸς Πισιδίᾳ καλουμένη, ἡ μὲν ἐν πεδίῳ κειμένη πᾶσα, ἡ δ' ἐπὶ λόφου, ἔχουσα ἀποικίαν Ῥωμαίων. ταύτην δ' ᾤκισαν Μάγνητες οἱ πρὸς Μαιάνδρῳ. Ῥωμαῖοι δ' ἠλευθέρωμαν τῶν βασιλέων, ἡνίκα τὴν ἄλλην Ἀσίαν Εὐμένει παρέδοσαν τὴν ἐντὸς τοῦ Ταύρου. ἦν δ' ἐνταῦθα καὶ ἱερωσύνη τις Μηνὸς Ἀρκαίου, πλῆθος ἔχουσα ἱεροδούλων καὶ χωρίων ἱερῶν. κατελύθη δὲ μετὰ τὴν Ἀμύντου τελευτὴν ὑπὸ τῶν πεμφθέντων ἐπὶ τὴν ἐκείνου κληρονομίαν.

T. 3. Strabo, XII, viii, 20:

Μεταξὺ δὲ τῆς Λαοδικείας καὶ τῶν Καρούρων ἱερόν ἐστι Μηνὸς Κάρου καλούμενον, τιμώμενον ἀξιολόγως. συνέστηκε δὲ καθ' ἡμᾶς διδασκαλεῖον

Ἡροφιλείων ἰατρῶν μέγα ὑπὸ Ζεύξιδος, καὶ μετὰ ταῦτα Ἀλεξάνδρου τοῦ Φιλαλήθους, καθάπερ ἐπὶ τῶν πατέρων τῶν ἡμετέρων ἐν Σμύρνῃ τὸ τῶν Ἐρασιστρατείων ὑπὸ Ἰκεσίου, νῦν δ' οὐχ ὁμοίως τι συμβαίνει.

T. 4. Athenaeus, II, 43 (ed. C. B. Gulick, Loeb Classical Library, 1927), talking about the waters of various places:

Τὰ δ' ἐν Καρούροις κατάξηρα καὶ σφόδρα θερμά. τὰ δὲ περὶ Μηνὸς κώμην, ἥ ἐστι Φρυγίας, τραχύτερά ἐστι καὶ λιτρωδέστερα, ὡς καὶ τὰ ἐν τῇ καλουμένῃ Λέοντος κώμῃ τῆς Φρυγίας. τὰ δὲ περὶ Δορύλαιον καὶ πινόμενά ἐστιν ἥδιστα. τὰ γὰρ περὶ Βαίας ἢ Βαίου λιμένα τῆς Ἰταλίας παντελῶς ἄποτα.

T. 5. Lucian, *Zeus Tragoedus* (ed. M. D. Macleod, Oxford, 1972, pp. 219-220), 8:

Ἡ Βένδις δὲ αὕτη καὶ ὁ Ἄνουβις ἐκεῖνος καὶ παρ' αὐτὸν ὁ Ἄττης καὶ ὁ Μίθρης καὶ ὁ Μὴν ὅλοι ὁλόχρυσοι καὶ βαρεῖς καὶ πολυτίμητοι.

T. 6. Lucian, *ibid.*, 42:

Πολλὴ γὰρ ἡ ταραχή, καὶ ἄλλοι ἄλλα νομίζουσι, Σκύθαι μὲν ἀκινάκῃ θύοντες καὶ Θρᾶκες Ζαλμόξιδι, δραπέτῃ ἀνθρώπῳ ἐκ Σάμου ὡς αὐτοὺς ἥκοντι, Φρύγες δὲ Μηνὶ καὶ Αἰθίοπες Ἡμέρᾳ καὶ Κυλλήνιοι Φάγητι καὶ Ἀσσύριοι περιστερᾷ καὶ Πέρσαι πυρὶ καὶ Αἰγύπτιοι ὕδατι. (Macleod's text, pp. 241-242, but reading Μηνὶ for Μήνῃ)

T. 7. Diogenes Laertius, VIII (ed. H. S. Long, Oxford, 1964), 34:

Ἀλεκτρύονος μὴ ἄπτεσθαι λευκοῦ, ὅτι ἱερὸς τοῦ Μηνὸς καὶ ἱκέτης. τὸ δ' ἦν τῶν ἀγαθῶν. τῷ τε Μηνὶ ἱερός. σημαίνει γὰρ τὰς ὥρας.

T. 8. Iamblichus, *Vita Pythagorae* (printed as appendix to the Firmin-Didot edition of Diogenes Laertius, Paris, 1878), 84:

Μηδὲ ἀλεκτρύονα λευκὸν θύειν. ἱκέτης γάρ, ἱερὸς τοῦ Μηνός, διὸ καὶ σημαίνουσιν ὥραν.

T. 9. Proclus, *Scholia in Platonis Timaeum*, IV, 251 C (ed. E. Diehl, Leipzig, 1906), talking about the propriety of worshipping various units of time:

Ἐπεὶ καὶ παρ' Ἕλλησι μηνὸς ἱερὰ παρειλήφαμεν, καὶ παρὰ Φρυξὶ Μῆνα Σαβάζιον ὑμνούμενον ἐν μέσαις ταῖς τοῦ Σαβαζίου τελεταῖς.

T. 10. *Orphic Hymns* (ed. W. Quandt, Berlin, 1962), Prooimion, 40-44:

Μητέρα τ' ἀθανάτων, Ἄττιν, καὶ Μῆνα κικλήσκω,/Οὐρανίαν τε θεάν, σύν τ' ἄμβροτον ἁγνὸν Ἄδωνιν,/'Αρχήν τ' ἠδὲ Πέρας, τὰ γὰρ ἔπλετο πᾶσι μέγιστον,/εὐμενέας τ' ἐλθεῖν κεχαρμένον ἦτορ ἔχοντας,/τήνδε θυηπολίην ἱερὴν σπονδήν τ' ἐπὶ σεμνήν.

TESTIMONIA ANTIQUA DUBIA

TD. 1. Clement of Alexandria, *Protrepticus* (ed. Potter, in Migne, *Patrologia Graeca*, Vol. VIII, col. 96; ed. O. Stählin, Leipzig, 1905, p. 19):

Οἱ μὲν γὰρ εὐθέως ἀμφὶ τὴν οὐρανοῦ θέαν ἀπατώμενοι, καὶ ὄψει μόνῃ πεπιστευκότες, τῶν ἀστέρων τὰς κινήσεις ἐπιθεώμενοι, ἐθαύμασάν τε καὶ ἐξεθείασαν, θεοὺς ἐκ τοῦ θεῖν ὀνομάσαντες τοὺς ἀστέρας. καὶ προσεκύνησαν, ἥλιον ὡς Ἰνδοί, καὶ σελήνην ὡς Φρύγες.

TD. 2. Hesychius, vol. II, p. 695, ed. Latte (Copenhagen, 1966); vol. III, p. 137, ed. Schmidt (Halle, 1858):

Ναὶ Μήν. ναί, Φρύγες.

TESTIMONIA ANTIQUA AD MENAGYRTAS PERTINENTIA

(See discussion *Berytus*, 17, 1967-68, p. 99)

T. 11. Hesychius, vol. II, p. 662, ed. Latte (Copenhagen, 1966); vol. III, p. 104, ed. Schmidt (Halle, 1858):

μηναγύρτης. ὁ ἀπὸ μηνὸς συνάγων [πανήγυρις].
This should probably be emended to: ὁ ὑπὲρ τοῦ Μηνὸς συνάγων or ὁ ἐπὶ Μηνὶ συνάγων.

T. 12. Suidas, vol. III, p. 387, ed. Adler (Leipzig, 1928-38):

Μηναγύρτης: ἀπὸ μηνὸς συνάγων.
Μηναγύρτης: ὁ τῆς Ῥέας ἱερεύς, ὁ κατὰ μῆνα ἀγείρων καὶ συναθροίζων.

T. 13. Athenaeus, XI, 472:

θηλυκῶς δὲ τὴν θηρίκλειον εἶπε Μένανδρος ἐν Θεοφορουμένῃ·
  μέσως μεθύων τὴν θηρίκλειον ἔσπασε.
καὶ ἐν Μηναγύρτῃ·
  προπίνων θηρίκλειον τρικότυλον μίαν.

T. 14. Stobaeus, *Florilegium*, vol. V, p. 769 f., nos. 100-101, edd. Wachsmuth and Hense (Berlin, 1912):

Μενάνδρου Μηναγύρτῃ·
Μακάριος ὅστις οὐσίαν καὶ νοῦν ἔχει.
χρῆται γὰρ οὗτος εἰς ἃ δεῖ ταυτῃ καλῶς.
  Οὕτω μαθεῖν δεῖ πάντα καὶ πλοῦτον φέρειν.
ἀσχημοσύνης γὰρ γίνετ' ἐνίοις αἴτιος.

T. 15. Ἀντιαττικιστής, ed. Bekker, *Anecdota Graeca*, I, p. 88 (Berlin, 1814):

Δεδιῳκημένα: Ἀντιφάνης Μηναγύρτῃ.

ADDENDA AND CORRIGENDA TO VOLUMES I AND II

A. Corrigenda to Vol. II

The following typographical errors in volume II are serious enough to warrant specific correction:

p. 11, line 10
"Weber" should be changed to "London".
p. 22, Nysa 9
For "Bust of Marcus Aurelius, r." read "Bust of Marcus Aurelius, l.".
p. 46, Silandus 3
For "Bust of Lucius Verus, r." read "Bust of Lucius Verus, l.".
p. 105, Apollonia Pisidiae 1
Add "r." to obverse description.
p. 121, Sagalassus 10
Reverse inscription Σαγαλασσέων inadvertently omitted.
p. 142, Sillyon 25
"Mabott" should be changed to "Mabbott".
p. 163, Laodiceia ad Libanum 3
"Fransiscanum" should be changed to "Franciscanum".
p. 172, line 12
"Descendantsa" should be changed to "descendants".
p. 176, AD 2, line 6
For "Antoin-" read "Antonin-".
p. 177, AD 3, line 9
For "Q(uititium)" read "Q(uiritium)".
Map — For "Sidibunda" read "Sibidunda".

B. I. Addenda to Volume I

Old material

Of the scatteredly published material found in Ramsay's 1912 excavations of the sanctuary at Antioch in Pisidia, the following dedication should be claimed for our subject. The attribution is not made so much on the basis of the conjectural restoration of the relief, as on that of the formula LVS.

A10. Three fragments of a marble stele. At the top preserved edge, there appear to be the remains of a bust of Men. The writing is said by Ramsay to belong to the first century A.D. Present location unknown.

Dimensions: unknown.

Bibliography: Ramsay, *JRS*, 6, 1916, pp. 94-95 and fig. 7; B. Levick, Roman Colonies in Southern Asia Minor, p. 117.

The stele bears the following inscription:
C. Anicius
Q. f. Ser(gia) Caesi-
anus, duumvir,
trib(unus) mil(itum) leg(ionis)
[III] Gallicae
[cum filia sua]
[A]nicia C. f.
[C]aesiana
[et matre sua]
[C]aesia
[P]rocilla
LVS

I am now informed that no. 27 is currently located in the Museo Gregoriano Profano, inv. no. 9937. Its dimensions are: height 110 cm.; width 74 cm.; depth, 54 cm. No. A8 is now published by E. Schwertheim, *Istanbuler Mittelungen*, 25, 1975, pp. 357-365. Reference is made to this interesting article in the notes to this volume.

New material

A11. Bronze figurine of Men, originally intended to be shown as equestrian. (The horse with which it is now associated is not origi-

PLATE I

A 8

C·ANICIVS
Q·F·SER·CAESI
ANVS II·VIR
TRIB·MIL·LEG
I·ITALICAE
· · · · · · · ·
ANICIA·C·F
CAESIANA
ET· · · · · · ·
CAESIA·R·
ROCILLA
L·V·S·

A 10

PLATE II

A 11

Prostanna 3

nal.) Men is shown with crescent, usual garb, and pine-cone in r. hand. Now in private hands.

Dimensions: Height 15.9 cm., including the substituted horse.

Bibliography: Sotheby-Parke Bernet Auction Catalogue, New York, 2, May 1975, no. 92.

II. ADDENDA TO VOLUME II

Prostanna 3
Obv.: Bust of Philip II, r., laureate.
Inscription: Αὐ... Μαρ. ᾽Ιου. Φιλιπ...
Rev.: Men standing slightly l., holding scroll (?) and pine-cone (?), in distyle temple. At his feet there are lions. On either side of his head, there is a rooster on a shelf. On each anta of the temple are five shields (?) of decreasing size from bottom to top, contrasting with the four shields (?) of Prostanna 2. (The number of these objects on Prostanna 1 is unclear.)
Inscription: Προστανγέων.

Bibliography: none.

Weight: 13.71 gr. (Wells).
Illustrated example: H. B. Wells Collection.

ADDENDA ULTIMA

To volume I — It is not out of the question that the statue described by R. Fleischer, *Artemis von Ephesos und verwandte Kultstatuen aus Anatolien und Syrien*, Leiden, 1973, p. 279 ff., with Plates 119-120, as "Göttin in Izmir," was actually intended to portray Men. The principal indication that this may be the case would be furnished by the crescent, traces of which are preserved at the shoulders, reinforced by the bucranium which appears on the "ependytes." The statue is reported to be from Selendi, ancient Silandus, where Men is known numismatically. Representation of Men with "ependytes" and the other characteristics of this type of statue, such as Zeus Labraundos of Mylasa or Zeus Helipolitanus of Baalbek (as well as a host of female divinities), would be unparalleled, but cannot be excluded. On the other hand, it must be remembered that the statue is very similar to the lunar Artemis Anaeitis of Fleischer, *op. cit.*, Pl. 39, which will be discussed below. A parallel for a male god with "Schleiermantel" is provided by the gem in Kassel, Fleischer, *op. cit.*, p. 385.

To p. 24, note 29 — Last but not least, we should note that in St. Matthew's account (2.12), when the wise men were warned not to go back to Herod, but to return by another way, the injunction took place κατ' ὄναρ. Interestingly also, the word χρηματισθέντες is used, reminding us of the phaseology of no. 129, which may not therefore be referring to anything more complicated than a dream.

To p. 25, note 34 — A fine example from Thessaloniki (*IG*, X, 89) is illustrated by G. Daux, *BCH*, 98, 1974, p. 538, fig. 6, with discussion and bibliography concerning this and other examples, pp. 547-8. The example illustrated uses the formula normal in Men-cult, κατ' ἐπιταγήν, rather than that commoner in Sarapis-cult, κατὰ πρόσταγμα. Prof. L. Castiglione promises a future volume on this subject in *EPRO*.

To p. 48, note 29 — In a letter of 28.1.1976, Mr. Francis Piejko suggests the following restoration in the penultimate line of mon. 121: .... καὶ τοὺς βωμοὺς [θυμιᾶν ὁμ]οῦ ......

This still encounters difficulties with the letter-traces which Bean claims to have seen, but seems to me to furnish the most satisfactory sense so far.

To p. 53 — The nearest parallel, within Asia Minor, to this idea of multiple gods, seems to be the double Aphrodite Kastneitis *Hellenica*, 11-12, 1960, p. 177 ff.

To p. 70 — A. E. Oikonomides, *Mithraic Art*, Chicago, 1975, pp. 47-49, discusses our monument no. 102. He opts for an origin of the monument in Britain, rather than its being a fairly modern import from Asio Minor. He also reads the following Ἀγαθόπο/υς Καουα Λή/νῳ εὐχὴν Μηνί and interprets Καουα as a genitive, the name of Agathopus' father, and a Celtic name. Lenus Men would also be a syncretism with a Celtic divinity, paralleled by Mars Lenus.

I am entirely willing to concede that ΚΑΟΥΑΛΗ may be the better reading for the second line — it is the reading given in the old line-drawing, whereas the photograph which I give shows the letters close to the relief to be rather unclear. Only a re-examination of the stone would settle the matter. I am not convinced, however, of Professor Oikonomides' interpretation, as it is totally unsupported by any known parallels, to say nothing of the inherent unlikelihood that a native Briton would give a Greek name to his son, who would then use Greek in his dedication. I continue preferring to see the epithet as geographical, and the monument, if originally British, as a dedication of a displaced Roman soldier or camp-follower.

Professor Oikonomides' interpretation, *op.cit.*, 53-56, of a relief from the Rhineland as showing a Men-Mithras, is without foundation, as the pine-cone is too widespread a symbol to base any identification on.

To p. 74 — For a gladiator named Petraites, of Neronian times, see Petronius, *Satyricon*, 52.3 and 71.6, as well as H. T. Rowell, *TAPA*, 89, 1958, pp. 14-24.

To p. 79, note 59 — Since completing the text, I have been able to see the work of B. Müller referred to in this note. He provides an interesting catalogue of gods who are designated μέγας, and of the documents in which the appellation occurs. On p. 327, he lists our *CMRDM*, I, nos. 67 and 83.

To p. 82 — For Artemis Anaeitis of Hypaipa, see R. Fleischer, *op. cit.*, pp. 185-187. The inscribed relief-stele which he publishes, p. 22, no. E71, with Pl. 39, shows an Artemis Anaeitis (from the Kula-area?) in essentially the guise of the Ephesian goddess, but with a moon-crescent, which also associates her with Men. The relief also shows a sun-god, and the inscription attests to an incantation cure. For the iconography of Artemis Anaeitis (who, incidentally, shares with Men the epithet Ἀξιοττηνή) and her relation to Men, as well as for various other valuable comments on the gods of this area, see Drexler, in Roscher's *Lexikon*, *s.v.* Mreter, cols 2865-68.

The monument cited from Buresch, footnote 4, is discussed by Drexler, *loc. cit.*, p. 199, with the indication that an illustration of it is given by G. Radet, *Cybébé*, Bordeaux, 1909, p. 85, Pl. 5, a work unfortunately unavailable to me at the time I wrote the text.

For the so-called Artemis Anaeitis of Apameia in Phrygia, see Fleischer, *op. cit.*, pp. 296-297.

To p. 83 — Demeter and Cybele, while both associated, with Men, seem to remain quite separate and distinct goddesses in this material. One should not forget, however, an important document of a much earlier period, the choral ode of Euripides' *Helen*, 1301 ff., in which a rather extensive syncretism of Cybele and Demeter is made. If this corresponds to any real religious phenomenon, and is not merely a flight of the poet's imagination, and if this syncretism remained alive in Roman-period Lydia, then it may have facilitated the associa ion of Demeter with Men through her identification with Cybele.

To p. 90, note 23 — In discussing associations of Men and Sabazius, it should not go unnoticed that Sabazius, too, is said to be the son of a mother goddess. Strabo states, in a passage also connecting Sabazius and Dionysus (X, iii, 15); τρόπον τινὰ τῆς μητρὸς τὸ παιδίον. In Lydia, Sabazius is customarily associated with Meter Hipta.

To p. 94, note 33 — The most recent treatment of Zeus Hypsistos I know of is that of J. M. R. Cormack, "Zeus Hypsistos at Pydna," *Mélanges Hélléniques offerts à Georges Daux*, Paris, 1974, pp. 51-55.

To p. 102 — Hans von Aulock's article, "Kleinasiatische Münzstätten, X", *JNuG*, 23, 1973, pp. 8-19, contains an exhaustive treatment of the coins of Parlais. Of importance for our subject are the following facts. 1) Herr von aulock disallows the two coins of Lucius Verus, which we have catalogued as Parlais 1 and 2. The former he reattributes to Antioch in Pisidia, where we should number it Antioch 27a, and the latter to the reign of Marcus Aurelius. Parlais thus disappears from the list of cities which copy the Antiochene type. 2) Aulock also prefers to see a lion, rather than a rooster, in the animal which accompanies Men on the coins of Parlais, but expresses no certainty about it. 3) The type which he singles out as type 15, in which Men is said to be looking back over his shoulder (the same example as I given for my illustration of Parlais 5) is probably simply an accident of wear, rather than a deliberate iconographical variant.

To p. 104, note 9 — The standard work on the subject of gods sacrificing is that of Erika Simon, *Opfernde Götter*, Berlin, 1953, which I was unfortunately unable to consult before completing the text. She is concerned with the theme in fifth-century vase painting and concludes that the gods are primarily propitiating other gods, and only secondarily setting models for humans. The relevance of her conclusions (she explicitly rejects the evidence of Plutarch) for beliefs of the Roman period is subject to doubt.

INDEX RERUM, VERBORUM, ET AUCTORUM NOTABILIORUM

Acts of the Apostles 79, note 61
Aedicula 2
Alia, material from 91
Alliance coins 44; 57; 85, notes 10, 11
Altar, represented on coins 104
Ameria, coin overstruck for 113, note 23
Anaeitis, Artemis Anaetis, Meter Anaeitis, Anahita 51; 82-83; 113
Ancyra, material from 46; 102; 106; (See also Galatia)
Anderson, J. G. C. 63-65, notes 38, 40, 46
Angels 25-26, note 36; 31; 69, note 14; 78; 90
Antioch in Pisidia 55-66; 86-87; and *passim*
Antiochene type 3; 56-57, note 10; 102-103; 105
Apameia, treaty of 55
Apolla, ancient place-name 40
Apollo 11; 50; 91-92
— Bozenos 21, note 18
— Helios Apollo Kisauloddenos 14; 85; 87; 91
— Lairbenos 91
— Nisyreites 74; 91, note 24
— Tarsios 33; 91, note 24; 85, note 9
Apuleius 26, note 37
Ares 85
Aristides, Aelius 18, note 4; 23-24, note 27; 40; 79-80
Artemis 60; 79; 82-83; 85; 96 (See also Anaeitis)
Asclepius 11; 24; 79; 84, note 8, 90
Asking the god a question 20, note 14
Athena 85
Attica, material from 1-16; 101-102; and *passim*

Attis 73; 82; 92-93, note 29; 95; 97
— as a proper name 73, note 32
— Menotyrannus 42, note 12; 73; 75-76, note 43; 93-94; 97-98
Attouda 13
Axe 85, note 9; 91, note 24; 99, note 2
Baby, Men shown as 6, 82, 99
Bakalakis, G. 3
Bean, G. E. 46-47, note 19
— and Mitford, T. 53, notes 44, 47; 88, note 17
Bömer, F. 8, note 32; 109; and *passim*
Brommer, F. 85
Bull, bucranium 9, note 37; 20; 87-88, note 16; 96; 102-105, notes 5 and 6; 108
Buresch, Karl 35, note 69; 37; 40, note 6
Cakes, as offerings 2, note 5; 111, note 12
Calder, W. M. 54; 72, note 26
Chairs, seats 46; 48-49, note 32; 65
Chickens 1-2; 101-102
Cilvastianus, epithet of Men 71
Cleanliness, ritual 9-11
Clement of Alexandria 86
Comana Cappadociae, material from 41
Communities, vows, etc., by or for 29; 39-40
Cornelia Antonia, worshipper of Men at Antioch 111-112, note 14
Couples, worship by, see Family
Crescents, with various unrealistic decorations 62
Cronin, H. S. 53
Cumont, F. 26, note 37; 52, note 37; 77, note 50; and *passim*
Curatores arcae sanctuarii 61
Cybele 73; 81-82; 93, note 29

INDEX

Dacia, material from 78; 107; 109
Deiotarus, king of Galatia 1; 73
Delos, material from 4; 7; 84; 109
Demeter 65; 83; 95
Deubner, L. 34
Dice-oracles 78; 94, note 31
Diogenes Laertius 102
Dionysus, Liber 7; 89-90; 96; 98; 105
Dioscuri 97
Dittenberger, W. 5; 15-16
Dreams 24, note 29
Drexler, W. 74-75; 107
Ears, of a god 78, note 55
Eger, Otto 27, note 39
Egyptian cults, see Sarapis, Isis
Eisele (first name?) 90
Epiphany-reliefs 1-2; 78
Epithets in genitive case 67-68, note 1
Eretria, material from 1
Etruscans 33
Eumenes, king of Pergamum 73, note 32
Eunapius 95
Eye-trouble 18, note 3; 20-21, notes 15 and 16
Facelessness, deliberate 54
Family, worship by 2; 59-60
Fehrle, E. 10
Fiscus 53, note 44
Foucart, P. 2-3
Frazer, P. M. 4
Funerary inscriptions 29; 51-54
Galatia 46; 73; 106
Grandjouan, C. 1, note 3; 101
Grapes 105
Gurlitt, W. 11, note 49
Gymnastic Contests 63-65, note 47; 83; 113
Hand, upraised as cult-gesture 38
Hasluck, Margaret Hardie 58
Hecate 26, note 37; 77; 84-85, note 9; 98, note 38
Helios, Sol 86, 92, 98 (See also Apollo, Pluto)
Hephaistos 97
Heracles 50
Hermes 26, note 37; 90-91; 97

Herrmann, Peter 18, note 3; 37
— and K. Z. Polatkan 32, note 52; 67, note 1
Hiller von Gaertringen, F. 4-5, note 24
Hittite etymologies 72, note 26
Iamblichus 102
Ilberg, G. 11, note 50
Isis 5; 7; 84; 97-98
Italikos, epithet of Men 34; 72-73
Italy 33; 72-73; 76
Ivy-leaves 62, note 36
Jewish influence on pagan religion 69, note 14; 79-80, note 64
Juliopolis, material from 87, 100
Keil, Josef 36, note 71; 67, note 1; 74, note 35; and *passim*
Kindling 12, note 57
Kore (Proserpina) 75, 79, 95, 98
— Kore Selene 87, 92
Kraabel, A. T. 12, note 56; 26, note 37; and *passim*
Krzyzanowska, A. 56
Kula, material from the area of 3, 74
Lamps 12, note 56
Laodiceia ad Libanum, material from 100-101
Lauffer, S. 6, note 30; 109, note 1
Letter-forms 5-6
Levick, Barbara 13-14, note 59; 49, note 30; 51, note 36; 57-58, note 12-13; 61, note 30; 111-112, notes 14 and 29; and *passim*
— and A. M. Davies 2, note 5; 111, note 12
Lions 101, note 4
Lucian 92, note 27
Luna as translation for *Men*, formula *LVS* 57-58, note 12; 63; 86
Luwian etymologies 68, note 11
Lycaonia-Cilicia, material from 51-54, 76-77
Lydia, material from 8-9, 14, 17-38, 43, 50, 72-73, 76, 110-111
Madness 20; 29; 91, note 25
Maeonia, city in Lydia 43
Magical papyri 26, 76, 94
Magnesia on the Maeander 16; 47,

note 23; 55-56; 89
Mao   113
Mausoleum of Halicarnassus   3
Menagyrtai   1; 110
Menander   9; 16
Mensis, as translation for *Men*   57; 87; 101
Military costume   106
Mischkowski, H.   14, note 63
Mithraeum, in Baths of Caracalla   41
Mithras   75; 78; 98
Mother   81-82; 90; 92; note 27
— Agdistis   50, 81
— Atimis   83
— Great Idaean Mother   98
— Hipta   21, notes 16-17
— Plastene   81
— Tarsene, Tazene   37; 81-82; 91
Multiple Mens   53-54
Mysteries, in Men-cult   36, 83
Nemesis   97
Neumann, G.   68, note 11; 72, note 26
Nock, A. D.   94
Nomenclature, Roman, at Antioch   112-113
Nysa ad Maeandrum, see Temple of Men at —
Oliver, J. H.   7, note 31
Orbius, Gaius   7, note 31
Origin of Men-cult   113-114
Orphic Hymns   92, note 27
Pan   6-7; 9; 88; 96
Panther   1; 3; 101
Parlais, material from   3; 102-103, note 5
Patera, held by Men   104
Perdrizet, P.   109
Perjury   27-29
Persian influence   34; 67-68, note 5; 83; 87-88, note 16; 102; 113-114
Pessinus, material from   92-93
Peterson, E.   79, note 63
Philodemus of Gadara, poet   34
Phrygia, material from   39-41
Piejko, F.   47-48, notes 23, 26-29
Pindar   25
Pine-cone   97; 104-105, note 11

Piraeus   2
Pleket, H. W.   18-19, note 8; 36, note 72
Pluto   75; 79; 95
— Pluto Helios   87; 92
Pollux, lexicographer   15, note 68
Polybius   73, note 32
Premerstein, Anton von   35; 67-68; 74, note 36; 85, note 9; and *passim*
Priest, of Artemis Anaeitis in Kula-area   34; 37; 110, note 6
— of Isis and Sarapis at Athens   5; 110, note 6
— of Men and other divinities, at Eumeneia   44; 50-51
— of Men (?), at Comana Cappadociae   41; 44
— of Men Askaenos and Hermes Agoraios, at Aphrodisias   44; 49-51
— of Men Askaenos, at Anaboura   44; 49; 51
— of Men Ouranios, at Andeda   44; 48-49
— of Men Patalaos (?), at Serivada   50, note 35
— of Men Toleseon (?), at Ormeleis   44; 49
Priestess, of great mother, in Piraeus   2
— of Men Axiottenos, in Kula-area   35; 37; 43; 51
Priesthoods, hereditary   37
— lifetime   37; 65
Priestly tribunals, hypothesis not necessary   31
Priests, of Men, at Antioch in Pisidia   65-66
Proclus   6, 90
Procurator et praegustator et a secretis Augusti   111
Prostanna, see Temple of Men at —
Radiate, Men shown   7; 42
Rainfall   6
Ram, sheep   1; 3; 97; 101
Ramsay, W. M.   13, note 61; 21, note 18; 41, note 7; 49, note 32; 58-59; 61; 68; 70, note 15; 91; 112,

INDEX

notes 16 and 20; and *passim*
Regling, K.   75, note 41; 86, note 13; 107
Repeated dedications   59
Reverse coin representations   96-97, notes 35-36; 107
Rhodes, material from   4-5; 7; 14; 110
River-god, Men as; rivers   6, note 29; 107
Riding, Men shown   99-100, notes 1-2
Robert, L., or J. and L.   2; 17, note 1; 25-26; 36; 46-47, notes 19 and 22; 64, note 47; 70; 75; 78-79, notes 53-55 and 58; 87; 94, note 31; 110-111; and *passim*
Roman fostering of Men-cult   33-34; 56; 64-65; 69; 72; 77; 113-114
Rooster, see Chicken
Roussel, P.   4
Ruge, W.   59-61, notes 19 and 31
Sabazius, Zeus Sabazius   21, notes 16-17; 90
Sacrifice   12-16
Saittae   26; 43; 79; 83; 95; 107
Samothracian mysteries   32, note 53]
Sarapis, Sarapeia   4-5; 7; 41-42, notes 11-12; 79, note 59; 84
Sardis, see Temple of Men at —
Savatra, place in Lycaonia   54
Schwertheim, E.   89, note 20; 93, note 29
Seated position, Men shown in   99
Selene   53, note 47; 63, note 47; 76, note 43; 86-88, note 16; 92, 95
Seleuceia, Claudioseleuceia, material from   105-106
Semitic influence, supposed, on Men-cult   26, 68-70, 74-75
Sevir Augustalis   111
Shield   100, note 2; 106, note 13
Siblia, material from   87
Sickness, as punishment for sin   19
Sin, moon-god of Carrhae   36; 58, note 12
Slaves, in Men-cult   8, note 32; 109-110, note 6
Sokolowski, F.   15, notes 66-68; 26,

note 37
Sounion, material from   7-16; 35-36
Staff or scepter, held by Men   104
Starry cap   92, note 27
Statue-base   2-3
Statues of one god dedicated to another   3, note 11; 81, note 1
Steinleitner, F.   22-23, notes 20-22, 24-26, and *passim*
Steles, subject to breakage   22-23, note 24
Stephanus of Byzantium   71, note 21
Strabo   21, note 17; 55; 58, note 13; 63, note 39; 67; 84, note 8; 86, note 13; 113
Summa rudis   111
Tables   13-14; 65-66; 102
Temple, of great mother, in Piraeus 2; 81, note 1
Temple, of Helios Apollo Kisaullodenos, at Smyrna   14
Temple, of Men, at Apollonia Pisidiae   44; 51
Temple, of Men, at Ayazviran   17; 43
Temple, of Men, in area of Burdur 44; 46-48
Temple, of Men, at Büyük Beşkavak 44-45
Temple, of Men, at Fassılar   44; 53
Temple, of Men, in Galatia (at Ancyra?)   44; 46
Temple, of Men, at Julia   44-45
Temple, of Men, at Nysa (and other material from the site)   44-45; 75; 85-86; 107
Temple, of Men, at Pisidian Antioch 13; 58-63
Temple, of Men, at Prostanna   3; 44-45; 101, note 4; 102; 106, note 13
Temple, of Men, at Sardis (and other material from there)   17; 43; 96, note 35; 107
Temple, of Men, at Sillyon   44; 51; 100
Temple, of Men, at Sounion; 7-16
Thasos, material from   5; 7

INDEX

Tlos 71, note 21
Tyche, Fortuna 44; 57; 85-86, note 13; 96
Victory, Men as god of 63, 66, 84, 106-107
Vidman, L. 4-5; 41-42, notes 9 and 11; 60, note 23; and *passim*
Wächter, Th. 10-11
Wide, S. 11, notes 50 and 52; 52, note 38
Wikander, S. 34
Wreath 62-63; 66; 106-107
Xanthus the Lycian, founder of Men-temple at Sounion 7-9; 109
Zeus 85; 88-89
— Ariou 24, note 30; 38, note 77; 67, note 1
— Benneus 40, 89
— hypsistos 94
— Killamenenos 71, note 18; 89
— Labraundos 91, note 24
— Masphalatenos 88-89; 92
— Ogmenos 89
— Ploutodotes 75; 77, note 51
— Soter 50, 89
— Trosou 67, note 1; 70, note 17
See also (Zeus) Sabazius
Ziehen, L. 11, note 49

Ἀγαθὸς Δαίμων 55, 94
Ἀεζηνοί 40
ἀγωνοθέτης 40, note 6; 65
ἀδέλφια 46-47, note 22
αἱρετίζω 8
ἀκρόαμα 16; 47, note 23
ἀκρόδρυα 16
ἀκροθίνιον 16
ἀκροκώλια 16
Ἀλιανῶν κατοικία 39
ἁμαρτάνω, ἁμάρτημα, ἁμαρτία 12, 19, 23, 51
ἀνακλιτήριον 46
Ἀνδρωνεινός 71
ἀνείκητος 42, note 10; 78
ἀνεπίλυτος 79
Ἀξιοττηνός 32; 51; 72; 101, note 3
— Ἀρτεμιδώρου 67
— ἐξ Ἀπολλωνίου 67
— ἐξ Ἐπικράτου 67

Ἄξιττα (Ἀξίοττα) 32, 72
ἁπλῇ τῇ ψυχῇ 9
ἀραί 28
Ἀρχελάου κώμη 33; 89, note 20
Ἀσκαηνός 32; 43; 49; 69; 72; 75; 84; 91; 101, note 3
Ἀσκαίη, Ἀσκανίη 32-33, 72
ἄσυλον 51, 100
ἀφιλοκέρδως 37
βασιλεύων 31-32; 39; 43
βωμός 17; 52, note 38
Γαλλικός 73; 75
Γάλλοι 73
Γοισηανός 71
Δόρου κώμη 33
δοῦλος 110-111
δοῦμος 14; 23; 34-35; 37-38; 110
δύναμις 30-31; 79
Δωλανός 70
ἐγ Διοδότου 67
ἔγγραφον 20
εἱργμός 48
εἷς (καὶ μόνος) θεός 78-80
ἐλεηθείς 19, note 10
ἐνορκῶ 52, note 39
ἐνχώριοι 40
ἐξ εἰδότων καὶ μὴ εἰδότων 22
ἐξ ἐπιταγῆς 23, 39
ἐπ' ἀγαθῇ τύχῃ 9, note 35
ἐπήκοος 42, note 10; 78
ἐπιστάτης 64
ἐπιφανής 25, note 31; 78
ἐρανισταί, ἔρανος 14-15; 46; 110
ἐφίερα 15
εὐείλατος 9; 30, note 44
εὐλογῶ 18; 30
εὐχαριστῶ 18
ζωγράφος 111
θεῖον 78; 95
θέμις 64
θεοὶ καταχθόνιοι 53; 77
θεοὶ Πισιδικοί 52, note 37
θεὸς Οὐινδιεινός 52; 70
θεὸς ὕψιστος 25; 49; 94
θησαυρός 48
θρεπτός 18, note 4; 60, note 20
θρησκεία 34, 37
θυρίς 47
ἱερόδουλος 21; 111, note 10

INDEX

ἱεροποίημα 18-19
ἱλάσκομαι, εἰλάσκομαι 19; 30
ἴχνη 25; 78
καθιερόω 26
καμάρα 75
Καμαρείτης 44; 68-69; 74-75; 77; 101, note 3
Καουαληνός 70
Κάρου 68; 101, note 3
κατ' ἐπίπνοιαν 26-27; 89
κατ' ἐπιταγήν 8; 22-24; 31; 89; 94
κατ' ὄναρ 24
κατὰ πρόσταγμα 89
κατακόπτεται 13, note 58
καταλουστικοί 9; 35; 37; 51; 90; 110
Καταχθόνιος 15; 53-54; 68; 75-77; 88
κατέχων 31-32; 39; 43
Κέρυζα 111
κολάζω, κόλασις 20; 21; 31
Κολιανοκωμήτης 71
κόλλυβα 15
κοπτοπώλης 2, note 5; 111
Κόρεσα 33
κύριος, κοίριος 23; 59; 69, note 14; 89
Κωμηνοί 40
Λαβάνας 68-69; 74
λαμπαδάρχης 50
λάρναξ 52, note 38
λύτρον, λυτρόω 21-22; 28; 36
λύω 28; 79
Μαξιμιάνειος 64-65
μέγας 79
Μηνιασταί 14; 110
Μοτελλείτης, Μοτυλείτης 70; 74
ναστός 15-16
ναυαρχήσας 60, note 23
ναυκόρος, νεωκόρος 35; 38; 41; 46, note 19
νέμεσις 21; 25
Ξένοι Τεκμόρειοι 13, note 59; 60-61
Ξευναγονηνός 71
ξυλικόν 47
ξυλοθήκη 48
οἰκονόμος 110
ὄμνυμι 28
ὁμολογῶ 30, note 44

ὅρκος 27, note 39; 28
ὅσιος καὶ δίκαιος 26; 78; 95
Οὐεζαεῖται 39
Οὐράνιος 49; 53; 76; 91
παιδίσχη 111
πάρεδρος 46
Πατάλαος 72
Πάτριος 64, 77
περίβολος 47
Πετραείτης 74-75; 90
πιττάκιον 27, note 39; 28
Πλουριστρέων 71
πραγματευτής 110
προκαθήμενος 36
πρόπυλον 17
προφῆτις 24, note 30; 38, note 77
...πυκηνός 72
Σεβαστὴ Εἰρήνη 50; 85
Σελμενηνός 40; 43; 70
σημαία, σημῆα 36
σκῆπτρον 27-29; 51
στηθύνιον 12, note 55
στηλογραφῶ 20; 30-31
στρωμνή 47, note 23
συμβίωσις 23; 34; 40, note 6; 110
συμβολαφόροι 36; 110
σχίζας 12, note 57
Σωτὴρ καὶ Πλουτοδώτης 41; 77; 95
σωτηρία 18; 40-41
Ταζηνῶν κατοικία 29; 39
Τάρσι 33-34
τεκμορεύσας 60-61; 66
τεκοῦσα 81-83
τέκτων 111
Τιάμου 23; 68; 72, note 26; 90
Τολισέων 71
τοπίαρις 110
Τουιτηνός 76
τράπεζα 13-14
Τυμωλείτης, -ος 52, 69, 72, 74
Τύραννος 8; 23; 31, note 47; 76; 89
ὑπηρεσία 20
Φαρνάκου 21, note 17; 67-68
φθορά 11
φράτρα 40, 110
Φωσφόρος 78
Χθόνιος 53; 77
χρηματισμός 49; 94

CONCORDANCE

of the items catalogued in the first two volumes and of the testimonia with the discussion in the third volume.

Item No.	Page in vol. III
1	1-3; 97, note 37; 101; 104
2	1-3; 38; 92; 97, note 37; 101
3	1-3; 97, note 37; 101
4	1-3; 101
5	1; 5-7; 88
6	1; 3; 5-7; 88; 107
7	1; 5; 7; 76; 84; 94; 110, note 6
8	4; 7; 8, note 32; 81, note 1
9	1-3; 8, note 32
10	1-3; 8, note 32; 38; 101; 104; 109
11	7-8; 76; 109
12	7-16; 76; 109
13	7-16; 76; 109
14	1-4; 101
15	5; 7; 18, note 5; 76; 89
16	4-5; 7; 109
17	4-5; 7; 55; 109
18	4; 7; 81, note 1; 84; 109
19	4; 7; 81, note 1; 89
20	71; 78; 109-110
21	78; 109-110
22	76; 93
23	76; 93; 98
24	76; 93; 98
25	76; 93; 98
26	76; 93; 98
27	76; 93; 98
28	3, note 11; 14; 21, note 17; 53, note 45; 76, note 47; 85; 87; 91; 95
29	3, note 11; 55, note 4
30	76; 97, note 36
31	18; 32, note 53; 67
32	18, 32, note 53; 76
33	18; 23; 32, note 53; 67; 110
34	3, note 11; 9, note 40; 35; 68; 74; 81, note 1; 90; 110
35	18-20, 23, 68, 82
36	76
37	18, 72

CONCORDANCE

Item No.	Page in vol. III
38	32, note 53
39	18, 38, 70
40	18
41	18; 41; 70; 77, note 51
42	23; 32, note 53; 33; 67; 74; 79; 81
43	28-30; 32; 59, note 19; 68; 73; 79, note 62; 82
44	17; 27-30; 32; 73; 79, note 62; 82; 91, note 25
45	18-19; 68; 82
46	18; 79
47	20-21; 24; 27; 32-33; 67; 91; 94
48	32, note 53
49	17; 23; 68; 83
50	9, note 37; 18-20; 23, note 24; 31-32; 94; 101, note 4; 102; 104-105
51	29-32; 68; 79; 83
52	17; 79
53	23; 34; 53, note 46; 68; 76; 79, note 62; 89; 92; 110
54	23; 34; 76, note 42; 89; 103; 105; 110
55	75
56	17; 44, note 16; 75
57	22; 36; 68; 83; 110
58	28-29; 32, note 53
59	18; 68; 83
60	18-19; 38; 68; 82
61	22-23; 76; 89
62	28-31; 74; 79, note 62
63	18-19; 38; 68; 79, note 62; 83
64	3; 6; 82; 99; 102; 105
65	17-18; 101, note 4; 105
66	22; 67; 105
67	28; 31-32; 74; 79; 81
68	18; 32, note 53; 74
69	20-21; 25-28; 33; 38; 79; 105
70	23; 32, note 53; 51; 62; 77; 107, note 14
71	23; 27, note 39; 28; 32, note 53; 51; 62; 77; 107, note 14
72	18; 32, note 53; 41; 77, note 51; 110
73	68
74	18; 68; 83
75	36; 83
77	19; 23; 30, note 44; 32, note 53
78	99
79	17; 43
80	18; 20; 27; 32, note 53; 110
81	52; 72
82	68

Item No.	Page in vol. III
83	76; 79; 95
84	3, note 11; 81
85	3; 23; 25; 78; 95; 97, note 37; 101; 110-111
86	3, note 11; 32; 67; 73
87	32, note 54; 40; 54; 99; 110
88	18, note 6; 39; 41; 77, note 51; 78
89	3, note 11; 77; 81, note 1; 84
90	22; 73; 105; 111
91	18, note 6; 41; 77, note 51; 99
92	18, note 6; 41; 76; 77, note 51; 91
93	23; 34; 39; 62; 72-73
94	76; 99
95	76
96	62; 71
97	39-40; 89
98	39-40, 71; 103, note 6
99	77; 84; 106
100	86, 92
101	32, note 54; 44; 50; 81; 84-85; 89; 91; 94
102	70; 103-105
103	44; 49; 71
104	54; 78; 99; 105
105	18, note 6; 32, note 54; 39-41; 77, note 51
106	32, note 54
107	18, note 6; 32, note 54; 40-41; 54; 70; 77, note 51; 99; 105
108	39-40; 70; 105
109	40; 70
110	62, note 37; 103, note 6; 107, note 14
111	44-45; 72
112	45; 99; 105; 106
113	45
114	45
115	45; 62; 71
116	45
117	45
118	32, note 54; 44; 50; 77; 84; 91
119	14, note 62; 32, note 54; 44; 91; 94
120	32, note 54; 44; 50; 91
121	14; 37, note 76; 44; 46-49; 53; 54
122	99
123	99; 103, note 6
124	54; 78; 99
125	54; 78; 99
126	31, note 47; 91-92
127	40; 54; 71; 105; 110
128	54; 99; 105
129	44; 48-49; 76; 94

CONCORDANCE

Item No.	Page in vol. III
130	32, note 54; 44; 51; 78
131	32, note 54; 44; 49-50
132	78; 94, note 31
133	78; 94, note 31
134	78; 94, note 31
135	78; 94, note 31
136	78; 94, note 31
137	103, note 6; 105
138	105
139	99
140	99; 104
142	6; 18, note 6; 41-42; 75, note 40; 77; 84; 95-97
143	52-53; 76
144	44; 52-53; 76
145	52-53; 76
146	52-53; 76
147	52-53; 76; 77, note 38
148	52-53; 76
149	52-53; 76
150	52-53; 76
151	52-53; 76
153	52; 70; 85; 96
154	52-53
155	52-54; 79
156	52-53; 76
157	71
158	46
159	46; 99; 105
160	56; 57-58, note 12; 111
161	63; 83
162	32, 59, 66, 72
163	13, note 60; 32; 65; 72; 111
164	63-65; 77; 83
165	63-65; 77; 83
166	63-65; 77; 83
167	63-65; 77; 83
168	63-65; 77; 83
169	63-65; 77; 83
170	63-65; 77; 83
171	63-65; 77; 83
172	63-65; 77; 83
173	63-65; 77; 83
174	63-65; 77; 83
175	56; 102-103
176	57-58, note 12; 59
177	9, note 37; 59; 60, notes 20 and 21; 61, note 30; 77; 102

Item No.	Page in vol. III
178	57; 63; 87; 113
179	59; 61, note 30
180	59; 60, notes 20 and 21; 61, note 30
181	59; 60, note 20
182	59; 61, note 31
183	59; 61, note 31
184	59; 60, note 20; 61, note 30
185	59
186	59; 112, note 15
187	59; 61, note 31
188	59; 61, note 30
189	59-60, note 20; 61, note 30
190	59
191	59, 60, notes 20 and 21; 112
192	59; 60, note 21; 60, note 30 and 31; 112, note 15
193	59, 60; 112, note 16
194	59; 60, note 20; 61, note 30
195	59; 61, notes 30 and 31; 62
196	59; 61, note 30
197	59; 61, notes 30 and 31
198	59; 61, note 30
199	59; 61, notes 29 and 30
200	57-58, note 12; 59; 61, note 30
201	59; 61, note 31
202	59; 60, note 20; 61, notes 30 and 31
203	59; 60, notes 20 and 21; 61, notes 30 and 31; 111
204	59; 60, note 20; 61, note 30
205	57-58, note 12; 59
206	59; 61, note 31
207	59; 61, note 30
208	59; 60, note 20; 61, note 30
209	59; 61, note 31; 62
210	59; 60, note 20; 61, note 30
211	59; 60, note 20
212	59; 60, note 21
213	57-58, note 12; 59
214	59; 61, notes 30 and 31
215	59; 61, note 31
216	59
217	59; 61, note 31; 111
218	59; 61, note 31
219	59; 60, note 20; 61, note 31
220	59
221	59; 61, note 31; 62
222	57-58, note 12; 59
223	59

CONCORDANCE

Item No.	Page in vol. III
224	59; 61, notes 30 and 31
225	59; 61, note 31
226	59; 60, note 20; 61, note 31; 113
227	57-58, note 12; 59-60, note 20; 61, note 31
228	59; 60, notes 20 and 21
229	59; 60, note 20; 61, notes 30 and 31
230	59; 60, note 20; 61, notes 30 and 31
231	57-58, 12; 59; 61, note 30
232	59; 61, note 31
233	59; 60, note 20
234	59, 112
235	59, 112
236	59; 61, note 30
237	59; 61, note 30
238	59; 61, note 30
239	59; 60, note 20; 61, notes 30 and 31
240	59, 60, note 21; 112
241	59; 60, notes 20 and 21; 61, notes 30 and 31
242	59; 60, notes 20 and 21; 61, notes 30
243	59; 60, note 20; 61, note 30
244	59; 60, notes 20-21; 61, note 30
245	59; 60, notes 20-21, 61, note 30
246	59; 60, note 21
247	59; 60, notes 20-21
248	59; 61, note 30
249	57-58, note 12; 59; 62, note 37; 107, note 14
250	57-58, note 12; 59; 62, note 37; 107, note 14
251	59
252	59; 60, notes 20-21
253	59; 60, notes 20-21; 61, note 30; 62, note 37; 107, note 14
254	59; 60, notes 20-21
255	13; 59; 65; 111
256	57-58, note 12; 59; 60, note 20; 111-112, note 14
257	57-58, note 12; 59; 60, note 30
258	59; 60, note 20
259	59; 60, notes 20-21
260	59; 60, notes 20-21
261	57-58, note 12; 59; 60, notes 20-21; 62
262	59-60, note 21
263	59; 60, notes 20-21; 64; 77
264	59; 60, notes 20-21; 61, notes 30-31
265	59; 60, note 21
266	59, 60, note 21; 61, note 30; 62, note 37
267	59; 62, note 37; 107, note 14
268	57-58, note 12; 59; 60, note 20
269	59; 62

Item No.	Page in vol. III
270	59; 60, note 20; 77
271	59; 60, note 21; 61, note 30; 62, note 37; 107, note 14
272	59, 60, note 21
273	59; 60, notes 20-21
274	59; 60, notes 20-21
275	59; 60, note 21
276	59
277	59; 60, note 20
278	59
279	59; 60, notes 20-21; 112
280	59; 60, notes 20-21; 113
281	59; 60, notes 20-21; 61, note 30
282	59; 62, note 37; 107, note 14
283	59; 60, notes 20-21; 62, note 37; 107, note 14; 111
284	59; 60, note 21
285	59; 62
286	59
287	59; 60, notes 20-21; 61, note 30; 62, note 37; 107, note 14
288	9, note 37; 59; 60, notes 20-21; 61, note 30; 62, note 37; 107, note 14
289	59-60, note 21
290	59; 60, note 21; 62, note 37; 64; 77; 111
291	59; 60, notes 20-21; 61, note 30; 62, note 37; 107, note 14
292	59; 60, note 21
293	59; 60, notes 20-21; 62, note 37; 107, note 14
294	59; 60, note 21
D 1	105
D 2	87, note 15
D 3	34; 76; 94
D 6	103, note 6
D 9	99
A 1	32; 67; 73; 79, note 62
A 2	18; 32, note 53; 38; 67
A 3	9, note 40; 24, note 30; 32, note 53; 37; 43; 110
A 4	59; 60, notes 20-21
A 5	9, note 36; 52-53; 76
A 6	9, note 36; 41; 44; 48; 59, note 19; 77, note 51
A 7	9, notes 35-36; 44; 70
A 8	26, 33, 76, 81-83, 89, 105
A 9	3, note 11; 50, note 35; 72
A 10	59; 112
A 11	99; 105
AD 1	102

CONCORDANCE

Item No.	Page in vol. III
AD 2	76; 93; 98
AD 3	76; 93; 98
AD 4	76; 93; 98
AD 5	52-54; 76
AD 6	52-54
AD 7	49, note 32; 65

Coins

Pharnaceia	1	106, note 13
Gangra-Germanicopolis	1	99
Juliopolis	1	87; 92, note 27; 99, note 2
,,	2	99, note 2
,,	3	99, note 2
,,	4	87; 92, note 27
,,	5	99, note 2
,,	6	87; 92, note 27
,,	7	92, note 27
,,	8	99, note 2
,,	9	104
,,	10	92, note 27
,,	12	104
,,	13	104
,,	14	92, note 27
Magnesia	1	84, note 8; 89-90; 106, note 13
,,	2	84, note 8; 89-90; 106, note 13
,,	3	84, note 8; 89-90; 106, note 13
,,	4	84, note 8; 89-90; 106, note 13
,,	6	104
,,	8	104
,,	9	103, note 6
Bageis	3	85, note 11
Gordus-Julia	2	101, note 4
,,	5	101, note 4
,,	6	101, note 4
,,	7	101, note 4
Nysa	4	44; 75; 101, note 3
,,	5	44; 75; 101, note 3
,,	6	44; 101, notes 3-4
,,	13	44
,,	18	44
,,	19	44; 85-96
,,	25	103, note 6
,,	28	103, note 6
,,	29	6, note 28; 44; 107
,,	30	64
,,	31	103, note 6
,,	32	103, note 6

Item No.		Page in vol. III
Nysa	33	103, note 6
,,	35	44; 85-86
,,	36	44; 85-86
,,	38	103, note 6
,,	40	44; 85-86
,,	41	44; 85, note 10
,,	42	44; 85, note 10
,,	43	44; 85, note 10
Saitta	3	107
,,	4	32, notes 53; 92, note 27; 101, note 3; 107
,,	5	32, note 53; 92, note 27; 101, note 3; 107
,,	6	32, note 53; 92, note 27; 101, note 3
,,	10	83
,,	13	83
,,	13	83
,,	17	107
,,	18	107
Sardis	1	32, note 54; 96, note 35; 101, note 3; 107
,,	2	32, note 54; 96, note 35; 101, note 3; 107
,,	3	32, note 54; 101, note 3; 107
,,	4	32, note 54; 101, note 3
Silandus	3	83
Attouda	1	13; 68; 92, note 27; 101, note 3
,,	2	92, note 27
Cidrama	1	103, note 6
Trapezopolis	1	104
,,	5	104
Accilaeum	1	103, note 6
Alia	1	106, note 13
,,	4	91; 99, note 2
,,	5	91; 99, note 2
,,	6	91; 99, note 2
,,	7	91; 99, note 2
Apameia	1	99, note 2
Cibyra	2	104
,,	3	104, note 7
,,	4	104
,,	5	104
Colossae	2	103, note 6
Eriza	1	99, note 2
Hadrianopolis	3	99, note 2
Hierapolis	1	103, note 6
,,	2	103, note 6
,,	3	103, note 6
,,	4	103, note 6
,,	5	103, note 6
,,	6	103, note 6
,,	7	103, note 6

CONCORDANCE

Item No.		Page in vol. III
Hierapolis	8	103, note 6
Hydrela	2	99, note 2
,,	3	99, note 2
,,	4	99, note 2
,,	5	99, note 2
Julia	1	99, note 2
,,	2	99, note 2
,,	3	57, note 10
,,	4	44-45; 103, note 6
Laodiceia	1	103, note 6
Prymnessus	1	92, note 27
,,	2	92, note 27
Sebaste	1	85, note 11
Siblia	4	57, note 10; 87; 103, note 5
,,	5	57, note 10; 87; 103, note 5
Temenothyrae	7	87
,,	8	87
,,	10	87
,,	11	87
Antioch	1	53, note 2; 92, note 27; 103
,,	2	53, note 2; 92, note 27; 103
,,	3	53, note 2; 92, note 27; 103
,,	4	53, note 2; 92, note 27; 103
,,	5	53, note 2; 92, note 27; 103
,,	6	53, note 2; 92, note 27; 103
,,	7	53, note 2; 92, note 27; 103
,,	8	53, note 2; 92, note 27; 103
,,	9	53, note 2; 103
,,	10	53, note 2; 92, note 27; 103; 106, note 13
,,	11	53, note 2; 103
,,	12	53, note 2; 92, note 27; 103; 106, note 13
,,	13	53, note 2; 92, note 27; 103; 106, note 13
,,	14	53, note 2; 92, note 27; 106, note 13
,,	15	53, note 2; 92, note 27; 106, note 13
,,	16	53, note 2; 92, note 27; 106, note 13
,,	17	53, note 2; 92, note 27; 106, note 13
,,	18	56; 102
,,	19	56; 102
,,	20	56; 103
,,	21	56; 103
,,	22	56; 97, note 36
,,	23	56
,,	24	56, note 8
,,	25	57
,,	26	57
,,	28	92, note 27
,,	37	57
,,	38	57

Item No.		Page in vol. III
Antioch	39	57
,,	41	92, note 27
,,	44	57
,,	48	57, 86
,,	51	57
,,	53	62, note 37
,,	56	57
,,	57	86
Apollonia	2	105
Ariassus	1	99, note 2
Baris	1	103, note 6
,,	2	100, note 2
,,	3	103, note 6
,,	4	100, note 2
,,	5	103, note 6
,,	7	103, note 6
Colbasa	1	103, note 6
,,	2	103, note 6
Conana	4	104
Lysinia	1	57, note 10; 103, note 5
Olbasa	1	100, note 2
,,	2	100, note 2
,,	3	100, note 2; 106
,,	4	100, note 2
Palaeopolis	3	103, note 6
,,	4	103, note 6
Pappa-Tiberia	1	103, note 6
Parlais	1	57, note 10; 102; 103, note 5
,,	2	103, note 5
,,	3	103, note 5
,,	4	103, note 5
,,	5	103, note 5
,,	6	103, note 5
,,	7	103, note 5
,,	8	103, note 5
,,	9	103, note 5
Prostanna	1	44-45; 101, note 4
,,	2	44-45; 101, note 4
,,	3	44-45; 101, note 3
Sagalassus	1	106, note 13
,,	4	103
,,	5	106, note 13
,,	6	100, note 2
,,	10	100, note 2
,,	19	92, note 27; 106, note 13
,,	26	100, note 2
,,	27	85, note 10
Seleuceia	1	105

Item No.		Page in vol. III
Seleuceia	2	105
,,	3	105
,,	4	105
,,	5	100, note; 105
,,	6	105
,,	7	100, note 2; 105
,,	8	105
,,	9	105
,,	10	105
,,	11	105
,,	12	100, note 2; 105
,,	13	100, note 2; 105
,,	14	105
Sibidunda	1	103, note 6
Timbrias	1	97
,,	2	103
,,	3	103
,,	4	103
Attaleia	1	103, note 6
Sillyon	1	100, note 2
,,	2	100, note 2
,,	3	103, note 6
,,	4	92, note 27
,,	5	100, note 2
,,	6	100, note 2
,,	9	100, note 2
,,	10	103, note 6
,,	11	103, note 6
,,	12	103, note 6
,,	15	100, note 2
,,	16	103, note 6
,,	18	104
,,	19	100, note 2
,,	20	100, note 2
,,	22	100, note 2
,,	25	100, note 2
,,	26	103, note 6
,,	28	92, note 27
,,	29	103, note 6
,,	30	92, note 27
,,	31	92, note 27
,,	32	92, note 27
,,	33	92, note 27
,,	34	103, note 6
,,	35	100, note 2
,,	36	100, note 2
,,	37	92, note 27
,,	43	100, note 2

Item No.		Page in vol. III
Sillyon	47	100, note 2
,,	49	92, note 27
,,	50	100, note 2
,,	51	100, note 2
,,	53	44, 100
,,	54	44, 100
Galatia	1	1, note 1
,,	2	92, note 27
,,	3	106
,,	4	106
,,	5	106
,,	6	106
,,	7	44; 46; 106
,,	8	44; 46
Ancyra	2	106
,,	3	46; 106
,,	5	46; 106
,,	6	104; 106
,,	7	57, note 10; 102; 103, note 5
,,	9	92, note 27
,,	10	57, note 10; 103, note 5
,,	11	104; 106
,,	12	104; 106
,,	13	57, note 10; 103, note 5
,,	14	103, note 6
,,	15	57, note 10; 103, note 5
Uncertain, perhaps Ancyra		56, 106
Pessinus	1	92
,,	3	104
,,	4	106
Laodiceia ad Libanum	3	100
,,	4	100
G 2		103, note 6
G 3		106, note 13
G 6		57, note 10; 102; 103, note 5
G 8		104, note 10; 106
G 12		104, note 10; 106
G 13		89–90
G 15		104, note 10; 106
G 16		92, note 27
G 17		71
Hildesheim plate		73; 92
T. 1		21, note 17; 58, note 13; 63, note 39; 67; 86
T. 2		21, note 17; 55; 63, note 39
T. 3		68; 84, note 8
T. 5		92, note 27
T. 7		102
T. 8		102

Item No.	Page in vol. III
T. 9	90
T. 10	92, note 27
TD. 1	86